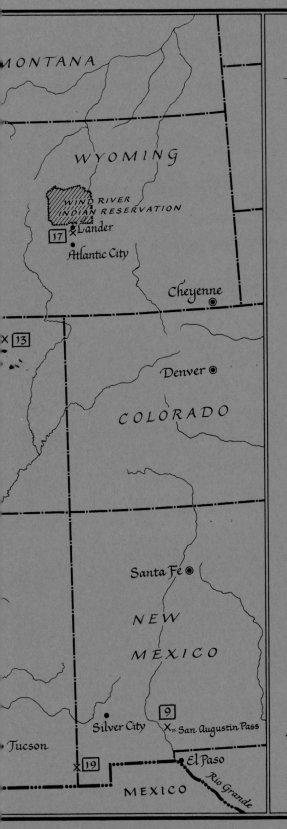

S0-BSX-944

LOST TREASURES

MONTANA

WYOMING

WIND RIVER INDIAN RESERVATION

17 ✗ Lander

● Atlantic City

Cheyenne ◉

✗ 13

Denver ◉

COLORADO

Santa Fe ◉

NEW

MEXICO

● Silver City

9

✗= San Augustin Pass

● Tucson

✗ 19

● El Paso

MEXICO

Rio Grande

A. Karl

Lost Treasures of the West

Lost Treasures of the West

Brad Williams

&

Choral Pepper

HOLT, RINEHART AND WINSTON
New York   Chicago   San Francisco

Library of Congress Cataloging in Publication Data
Williams, Brad.
        Lost treasures of the West. *New York: Holt, 1975,*
183p.
1. Treasure-trove—The West.   2.   Legends—The West.
I. Pepper, Choral, joint author.   II.   Title.
     F591.W719   917.8′03′2   74–5127
          ISBN 0–03–013186–3

First Edition
Printed in the United States of America

CONTENTS

Lost Treasures
of the West

INTRODUCTION

There have been hundreds of books written about lost treasures and mines of the West. Most of these books derive from death-bed confessions or revelations by grizzled prospectors or remorseful murderers who invariably manage to gasp out the story of the treasure but expire in the arms of a friend or doctor before they can pass on anything but the most meager clues to its location.

In this book, as in our previous books, we have avoided this approach to the tales of treasure. Although we have not written this work with the attitude of dedicated historians, there is tangible evidence as to the existence of treasure in each of the following stories. Thus, if the reader wishes to pick up a metal detector or a scuba tank and go seeking, he may do so with the knowledge that what he seeks is not entirely based on fantasy. However, the writers admit candidly that in most of these tales there is the probability that somewhere in the story the facts have been augmented by legend. For example, at the time the *Brother Jonathan* sank at the entrance to Crescent City Harbor in California, it was reported to be carrying approximately $500,000 in gold dust and gold nuggets. Now, a little more than a century later, there are few people in Crescent City who do not know for a fact that the side-wheeler went

1

down with more than $2 million in precious gems, currency, and gold bullion on board. The increased value of the treasure is not based upon the inflated value of gold. It stems from the expansion of a legend over the years.

Inflation does increase the value of a treasure, however. A diamond that sold for $1,000 in the late thirties might well bring ten times that amount today. With this in mind we shall make an exception immediately to our ban on deathbed confessions and tell a story about diamonds that came from the late Jake Ehrlich, the well-known San Francisco criminal attorney.

Shortly before the outbreak of World War I in Europe, a young Frenchman named Antoine Rosselet decided that the odds on his reaching middle age would be much better if he avoided military service by migrating to the United States. Arriving in San Francisco a few months later, he went to work as a waiter in one of the city's better restaurants. When he was twenty-eight, he met and married Helen Riley, a pretty young girl ten years his junior. A few months later the romance was over. Before Helen was twenty, she literally was not speaking to Antoine, nor was he speaking to her. They communicated with each other only by note, and although their mutual hatred intensified during the ensuing months and years neither husband nor wife, because of religious beliefs, sought a divorce as an answer to their problem.

They lived modestly. Rosselet saved his money, and shortly after the United States entered World War I he opened his own restaurant. Apparently it was a success, but the bonanza for Rosselet came with the passage of the Volstead Act. He opened one of the best speakeasies in the city where he served fine liquor and wines with good food. He also became active in the illegal importation of liquor from both Canada and Mexico, and the profits from bootlegging and his restaurant made him rich.

With the repeal of Prohibition, Rosselet closed his restaurant. The Depression was at its lowest ebb, and there were few who could afford his cuisine. He bought a small bar on the North Beach, anglicized his name, apparently to avoid the stigma of his rum-running days, and moved with the bitter and noncommunicative Helen into an upper-middle-class section of the city. His bar prospered, not to the extent that his restaurant had during the Prohibition era, but enough so that he did not have to dip into his capital.

In 1948 Rosselet was informed by his doctor that he had a brain tumor and that his life expectancy was only a matter of a few months. Rosselet was approaching sixty. For thirty years, almost half of his entire life, he had been married to a woman to whom he had not spoken a word. He hated her. Yet, he believed that under the California community property laws, his wife would inherit everything he owned, no matter what kind of will he left. There was no way to prevent her from getting possession of their house. She was aware of a small insurance policy and, of course, she knew about the bar. Because of their peculiar relationship, however, she did not know that her husband was worth approximately three-quarters of a million dollars. This money, the dying Rosselet decided, would never cross the palms of Silent Helen.

He sold his bar, cashed in his stocks and bonds, and with the proceeds he quietly bought $750,000 worth of diamonds. Then he was faced with a dilemma. If he put his hoard in a safe-deposit box, Helen certainly would find it after his death. He had no relatives or friends close enough to trust with such

3

a fortune. He had no plans for disposition of the money after his death other than a passionate desire that his wife not get it. As a temporary solution to his problem, he placed the precious stones in a large metal box, then buried them in the backyard of his home when Silent Helen was out of the house.

A few weeks later Rosselet collapsed and was taken to a hospital. Apparently he realized that his hold on life was tenuous, and so, rather than taking his secret to the grave with him, he told the doctor what he had done, adding that the doctor could have the treasure any time he could get it.

The doctor accepted the offer appreciatively and discreetly. A few days later, Rosselet died. The doctor went to the house to offer his condolences to the widow. Apparently he decided to wait until she too passed on, then return to pick up his inheritance without the bother of a probate.

In the fall of 1965, while Silent Helen was enjoying perfect health and still living in the same house, the doctor suffered a mild heart attack. He consulted with Jake Ehrlich, an excellent investigative attorney about his will, and during the conversation he mentioned the peculiar bequest from Rosselet. He identified the donor only by his French name, but he did describe part of his background.

A few weeks later, the doctor, his wife, and his son were killed in a freeway accident in Los Angeles.

The most difficult part of Jake Ehrlich's investigation was finding the court order through which Rosselet changed his name. When Ehrlich discovered the doctor's name on Rosselet's death certificate, he knew he had found the man. The lawyer went to Rosselet's house where his widow still lived.

She was a small woman, very spry and charming. Ehrlich

4

found it difficult to reconcile her with the Silent Helen described by the doctor, but she made it quite clear to the lawyer that she had found life much more enjoyable since her husband's death. She was not the least bit interested in selling her house.

"Every day I read the obituaries," Ehrlich told one of the authors of this book early in December 1971. "When I read that this very nice little old lady has passed on to her reward, I'm going to buy that house. Those diamonds are probably worth two million by now."

"What if someone else has the same idea?" he was asked.

"That could be," Ehrlich replied. "All the clues to this treasure are in the court records. You just have to know where to look."

A few days before Christmas in 1971, Jake Ehrlich suffered a fatal heart attack in his Nob Hill apartment. His death was front-page copy for the San Francisco newspapers. It is quite possible that Silent Helen may have been reminded of Ehrlich's offer to buy her home when she read of his death, but it is unlikely that she knew of the treasure in her backyard.

Maybe Silent Helen is still alive. Maybe her house has withstood the onslaught of the high-rise apartments in San Francisco. Maybe she will read this book and learn of the treasure her husband buried in her backyard. If this happens, all that will remain for her to do is to obtain a metal detector and run it over her property. Possibly it has already been found and quietly cashed, but if it has, the writers have been unable to find any record that this is the case.

Some of the lost treasures described in these tales may have been found. In other of the tales, such as the shipwreck on Nehalem Spit, a part of the treasure is known to have been recovered and is the best clue to the location of the rest of the fortune.

We have chosen little-known legends of lost treasure and we have told you where to look.

Los Angeles, California   *Brad Williams and Choral Pepper*
June 1973

BEESWAX AND BULLION

When Lewis and Clark reached the end of their long overland trek at the mouth of the Columbia River, they were given a large chunk of beeswax by a group of welcoming Clatsop Indians. History does not record what these two explorers did with their gift, but if they had realized its significance they probably would have made a beeline to its source.

The beeswax came from one of the most spectacular areas of the Oregon coast, some thirty miles south of where the Columbia River pours into the Pacific Ocean in what is known today as Nehalem Beach, Oregon. Immediately to the south of Neahkahnie Mountain, the beach is adjacent to the Nehalem River on a wild spit of land covered only by shifting sand dunes and large clumps of sea grass. There is nothing there that would appeal to a busy Oregon bee even if he had the strength to fight the steady prevailing offshore winds.

This beeswax, which still can be scavenged by beach-combers, was manufactured by bees in India almost three centuries ago. Its presence on this remote Oregon beach probably solves the mystery of what happened to a huge Manila galleon that vanished in 1705 with a cargo of millions of dollars worth of gold, silver bullion, and precious gems.

The name of the galleon was the *San Francisco Xavier*. Built in 1691 in Cavite, in the Philippines, it was approximately 175 feet long, 50 feet wide, carried 80 guns and, when fully loaded, about 1500 tons of cargo. If it was built like most of the other Manila galleons, its frames were made of teak, and the other parts of the ship were constructed of Philippine hardwoods such as *lanang* and *molave*.

For more than two hundred and fifty years, the Manila galleons operated a regular route between Manila and Acapulco. Usually one ship traveled in each direction once a year. The westbound ships headed south from Acapulco to pick up the prevailing winds and current near the equator, then north as they neared Guam, an island which the Spanish named Los Ladrones (The Robbers) because of the light fingered habits of the natives. The galleons usually paused here to reprovision their stores before continuing on into Manila.

Eastbound ships headed north to catch the prevailing winds and the Japanese current, usually turning east at the northern end of Japan for the long voyage across the Pacific. Landfall of the North American continent varied anywhere between the thirtieth and forty-fifth parallel or, roughly, between the northern coast of Baja and the northern coast of Oregon. More often than not, landfall was made far enough north so that the galleons could put into either Monterey or San Francisco for reprovisioning.

Westbound, the galleons carried unexciting cargos of cocoa, chocolate, and similar products, plus cash. Diocesan records indicate that the *San Francisco Xavier* carried 2,070,000 pesos in 1688. When voyaging back to Acapulco, however, the cargoes were much more exotic.

William Lytle Schurz, in his book *The Manila Galleon* reports that the ships carried silks, taffeta, and delicate Cantonese crepes from China, rich vestments for the churches in New Spain, and gauzes, napkins, and handkerchiefs from the Mogul Empire of India. Persian rugs imported into the Philippines from India and the Malabar and Coromandel coasts were very much in demand.

No galleon ever departed for New Spain from Manila without large shipments of gold and silver bullion and precious stones. One cargo manifest from a galleon that arrived in Acapulco in 1767 lists diamond earrings, necklaces, pendants, and bracelets by the hundreds, a large diamond-encrusted cross, sword hilts studded with jewels, and thousands of uncut or unset precious stones. No vessel ever made the trip without a large shipment of Ghedda beeswax, made in India, and much in demand in New Spain for use as votive candles and for lighting.

The galleons were known to have carried another cargo: slaves brought to the Philippines from the east coast of Africa. The traffic in slaves was small, but each passenger aboard ship was permitted to have two personal servants. Often these were blacks and were sold by the passenger when the galleon arrived in Acapulco.

From the first crossing in 1565 to the last in 1815, there was a record of thirty Manila galleons lost on the westbound trip. Most of these foundered in the turbulent straits of the Philippines. One went aground on the coast of Japan, another was captured by English freebooters, and still another broke up on the northern edge of San Miguel Island off the California coast. Of these lost galleons, only two vanished without a trace: the *San Francisco Xavier* and the *San Antonio*. There are some reports, however, that the *San Antonio* was the galleon lost at San Miguel. If this is true, it leaves only the *San Francisco Xavier* unaccounted for, and there is considerably more evidence than several tons of beeswax to indicate that this long lost Manila galleon may be resting under one of the sand dunes on Nehalem Spit in Oregon.

It is not an improbable location for the *San Francisco Xavier* to have been battered ashore by an early fall storm. Nehalem is a very short distance above the forty-fifth parallel, which was the northernmost point of a Manila galleon's eastern route. The Nehalem River enters the ocean here, and the spit curves upward at the river mouth to form Nehalem Bay. It would have been possible for a galleon seeking sanctuary from a storm in this sheltered water to have been blown or pushed ashore on the Nehalem Beach by the river's currents.

The tons of wax that have been picked up on Nehalem Beach are the strongest clue that the *San Francisco Xavier* was wrecked there. Beeswax is virtually indestructible, except by heat, and the Oregon beaches are always cool. It is still used in the manufacture of votive candles because of its higher melting point and slow burning characteristics. The origin of beeswax can easily be determined through analysis. European, Japanese, and North American beeswax is manufactured by the common bee, *apis mellifica*. Beeswax from India, which is the slowest burning of all, is made by the bee known as *apis dorsata*. This Indian beeswax is commonly called Ghedda wax and it was used in the seventeenth century by the churches and the rich of Mexico City and Guadalajara. Analysis of the beeswax found on Nehalem Spit shows it to be Ghedda wax.

The wax also was "sized" to the proportions required by a Manila galleon, and vast numbers of the pieces bear numerals and letters which have been interpreted by some scholars to be the equivalent of a modern bill of lading.

The Clatsop Indians told Lewis and Clark that the beeswax came from a shipwreck, and, according to a legend that has been passed on for centuries, some of the men on board the doomed ship survived. Most of the survivors set off toward the south. Among those who made it to shore successfully was a giant black man.

The late Senator Richard L. Neuberger of Oregon, who was an avid historian of the Pacific Northwest, was fascinated by the beeswax and its possible origins. He told of one variation of a Clatsop Indian legend which goes back to the shipwreck and involves a gigantic Negro.

According to Neuberger, the black giant and a white man were the only survivors of the shipwreck on Nehalem Spit. The day after the storm subsided, the giant, who was apparently the white man's servant, went back out to the wave-pounded wreckage of the ship and presently returned carrying a large chest. The giant and his companion then proceeded to bury the chest well above the tide line and away from the spit, marking the site with a triangular placement of large rocks. Then the pair set off to the south. They had covered only a short distance when they ran into a group of hostile Indians and were murdered.

Early in the 1930s, a farmer named Edward G. Calkins turned up a skeleton while he was plowing a field near Three Rocks Beach, only a few miles south of Nehalem in Oregon. A short time later, after some careful digging, he discovered two skeletons, and one was that of a giant about 8 feet tall. A delayed autopsy showed that both men had been murdered by blows to the head more than two hundred years earlier. The skeleton of the giant was that of a Negro.

In her book, *Lost Mines and Treasures of the Pacific Northwest*, Ruby El Hult, tells of a discovery by Pat Smith, a beachcomber, at Nehalem in 1898. Combing the beach after a heavy storm, he came across the remains of an ancient ship, bared by the shifting sands on Nehalem Spit. The frames were made of teak, the same wood used in the construction of the Manila galleons. After he salvaged several pieces of the wood, which he fashioned into canes and sold as souvenirs, Smith was convinced the wreck was that of a Manila galleon and made several attempts to get into the hold areas. All proved futile because of the shifting sands. A short time later another storm buried the wreckage once again under the dunes.

The shipwreck surfaced once again after a heavy storm in 1929. This time the galleon remained in view a sufficient time to attract the attention of Phillip I. Cherry, the British vice-consul in Astoria, Oregon. Cherry knew of the incredible value of a Manila galleon's cargo, and, after a close inspection of the wreck, he attempted to interest a salvage company in raising the hull.

The year 1929, however, marked the start of the Great Depression. To raise the hull of the ancient ship would have required the construction of a $30,000 cofferdam. Cherry could induce no one to risk that much money in those parlous times.

The shipwreck still lies on Nehalem Spit. The ribs of the vessel are bared occasionally after a storm, sometimes for a few hours only, sometimes for months before they are again inundated by the sand.

The legend of the buried treasure chest has many variations and has attracted more treasure seekers than the lost galleon. More than one thousand holes have been dug around Neahkahnie Mountain in quest of a treasure chest, which contains only a tiny part of the treasure left on the galleon. However, if the wreck is the remains of the *San Francisco Xavier*, there's a fortune in gold bullion, silver, and precious gems in those sand dunes.

There is even a greater treasure in the wreckage of the other lost Manila galleon, the *San Antonio*, which is believed by many to be the one that foundered on the western side of San Miguel Island, a few miles off the California coast.

The island lies approximately thirty miles south of Point Concepcion. Shaped roughly like a triangle, it is about 9 miles long and 5 miles broad at its widest point. Technically, it does not belong to the United States despite its geographical position some two hundred miles north of the Mexican border. It is one of the so-called Channel Islands, none of which were mentioned in the treaty by which the United States acquired California from Mexico, a point brought up at regular intervals by Mexican politicians. The U.S. State Department never has debated the matter seriously with our southern neighbor because neither country really cares who has the title to the unpopulated and barren Channel Islands, except for Santa Catalina Island.

San Miguel is the most mysterious of the eight Channel Islands. It is a barren, windswept place, haunted by ghosts of prehistoric tribes. There is a legend that any man who attempts to make it his home is doomed to die violently. It is here that Juan Rodriguez Cabrillo, who many believed was the first conquistador to sail up the California coast, is reported to have been buried. It is a graveyard for many ships including the *San Sebastian*, which sank in 1754, the *J.F. West* which crashed into its hostile shores in 1889, the *Comet* in 1911, and the *Cuba* in 1923. It also is the probable site of the wreckage of the *San Antonio*.

13

In the year 1603, the Chinese and the Filipinos in Manila joined in a massive revolt against the Spaniards. At the start of the revolt, the *San Antonio* was in port and preparing for its return trip to Acapulco. In addition to the regular cargo, most of which had already been loaded, the captain suddenly found that his ship had become the sanctuary for the families, with their valuables, of the leading Spanish politicians. Millions of dollars in precious stones, jewelry, cash, and bullion were carried on board the galleon by refugees. More valuables were loaded to be shipped to the New World where the political climate was believed to be more stable.

When the *San Antonio* left Manila it carried more riches than any other galleon in the entire two hundred and fifty years of the run. It was never heard of or seen again. Spanish historians state flatly, however, that the *San Antonio* was wrecked upon the treacherous west shore of San Miguel Island, and there is strong evidence to support this contention. Visitors to the island have found lumps of Ghedda wax on the western side of the island. Like the *San Francisco Xavier*, the *San Antonio* carried a large shipment of this Eastern beeswax.

The area to search is small, but the breakers will thwart the efforts of any scuba diver.

THE NAIL ON THE HEAD

The wagon trains usually gathered in Fort Boise, Idaho, to reprovision and rest up for the final trek along the Oregon Trail into the lush valleys of western Oregon, but rarely were there so many wagons in the outpost as in the midsummer of 1845. In the early part of August, six wagon trains, comprising a total of three hundred wagons, about one thousand adults, twenty-three hundred cattle, eight hundred oxen, and one thousand goats were straining the hospitality of Fort Boise as preparations were made for the last segment of the long trip over the Blue Mountains and down the banks of the Columbia River.

Five of these wagon trains had been made up in Missouri; the sixth originated in Iowa. The land voyage across the plains and over the Continental Divide had been long and dull. Without exception, all of the travelers were eager to reach their destination, and, thus, most were easy marks for a persuasive promoter of indeterminate age named Stephen Meek when he offered to guide them over a 200-mile shortcut to Oregon's Willamette Valley for a five-dollar fee per wagon. If there had been no Meek, there would be no legend of the lost Blue Bucket gold. Today there is a plethora of versions about the lost Blue Bucket, all versions verifying that the whole affair started with Meek.

One of the wagon trains was commanded by William G. T'Vault from St. Joseph, Missouri, a man who, either by luck or cunning, proved to be the smartest wagon master in Fort Boise at this time. Of the six commanders, only T'Vault resisted the blandishments of the smooth-talking Meek. The other wagon masters collected the five-dollar fee from the members of their train, gave the money to Meek, then lined up to follow him into disaster.

The huge wagon train started west from Fort Boise as a unit. Then, on August 24, it split into two parts. T'Vault, with about one hundred wagons, continued along the well-established Oregon Trail; the other two hundred wagons followed Meek to the south.

For the first day or two the Meek contingent found the way passable. Then the trail gradually disappeared under a mass of boulders which shattered wheels and pounded the hooves of the cattle so severely that many could not stand. The heat grew intolerable and tempers strained to the breaking point. Meek said the boulders were the result of some unknown natural phenomenon that had occurred since he had last used the trail.

Two weeks later the battered wagon trains came down from the mountains into the smoother, but more deadly, parched alkali plains northeast of Malheur Lake in an area known today as Crane Prairie. The caravan paused beside a spring, but the water was too polluted to drink. Even the

16

cattle refused to touch it, and some literally were dying of thirst.

The wagon train commanders called an emergency meeting with Stephen Meek, who finally admitted that he was indeed lost. Shortly after this meeting Meek disappeared. There are two versions of his disappearance. The more charitable states that Meek sought sanctuary in one of the wagons and that he escaped some weeks later. The other version reports that Meek was shot and quietly buried without the usual services, for there were no mourners. A week later, as the caravan struggled across the desert, it stumbled upon a series of small sloughs that contained stagnant but potable water. They named the area Stinking Hollows, a name it still bears, and here the immigrants made camp.

Mostly sick, more than one thousand men, women, and children, approximately two thousand cattle, five hundred oxen, and eight hundred goats crowded into the sloughs. It was here that the first victim of Meek's mistake, a woman named Mary Smith, was buried. The following day a young boy died.

Scouting parties were sent in search of water and, within a few days, one of the scouts returned with news of a spring some forty miles to the north. Camp was struck and the caravan moved on.

There is an interesting sidelight to the encampment at Stinking Hollows. The tale may be apocryphal, but many years later an Indian told a newspaper reporter in The Dalles, Oregon, that when he was a small boy he had, on several occasions, crept to within a few yards of the immigrants and watched them. He knew that several of the travelers were dying of thirst, and he also knew the location of a large spring within an hour's ride of the camp.

"Why didn't you tell them about it?" he was asked.

"I couldn't," the Indian replied. "I was an Indian and would have been shot before I could have told them."

The spring found by the scouts was in the foothills of the mountains, not far from the headwaters of Crooked River. The water in the small spring was crystal clear but was far from sufficient to slake the thirst of the wagon train that descended upon it. It was in an area covered by juniper trees and splattered streams of lava from some prehistoric volcanic eruption. Dry creek beds wandered throughout the lava potholes. Once again the wagon train came to a halt as the scouts explored for a way out of the dilemma. The water shortage began to take its toll. On September 23, four persons died. On the following day, six more died. Another half-dozen perished in the ensuing six days. The wagon masters broke camp and struggled on.

On the last day of the month a small girl died. Each wagon in the train was, of necessity, self-sufficient, and the mother of the small girl had no time to mourn. The wagons paused only long enough to dig a grave, then moved on. Late in the afternoon the train came across another lava flow. As the wagons struggled over this, there was a sudden desert cloudburst. The dry wash became a flowing stream for only a short time, but even when the water seeped through the gravel, enough remained on the surface in the potholes of the lava to warrant making camp for the night.

The husband of the bereaved mother was a drunkard. He had been in varying degrees of intoxication ever since he left Fort Boise, and not a night went by in which he did not drink himself into a stupor. This night was to be no exception. While the wife prepared the evening meal, her husband opened a fresh bottle of whiskey. Their ten-year-old son picked up a small blue bucket, ran over to the bank of the creek bed, and presently began collecting small pebbles, tossing those that appealed to him into his bucket. The husband upended the whiskey bottle several times, belched, then sullenly told his wife to get out of his sight and into the back of the wagon, which she did. Her son then returned and climbed into the wagon. As the boy entered the wagon, the flap was pulled back and the woman saw her husband eating alone, swilling all of the food down with his whiskey. Later, as it grew dark, she watched her husband stretch out on the ground, a fist clenched around the neck of his nearly empty whiskey bottle. She crept down from the wagon, started the fire again, and prepared another meager meal for herself and her son.

Much later that night, while everyone in the caravan slept, the woman once again climbed down from the wagon. In her hands she carried a hammer and a long thin nail. She moved quietly toward her husband, knelt down beside him, placed the point of the nail against his skull, and drove it into his head with one powerful blow of the hammer. Then she covered up the head of the nail with his thick and matted hair and crawled back into the wagon.

There was no autopsy the following morning when his body was discovered. There had been too many deaths and if any thought at all was given to the cause, it probably was attributed to alcoholism. He was buried, and a pile of stones was left behind to mark his grave. No one knew how he died until some thirty years later when his widow made a deathbed confession to her son.

The day after his death an advance party returned to the caravan with news that the Deschutes River was only two days' journey away. A week later the wagon train arrived safely in The Dalles. The widow and her small son settled in an area

19

of the Willamette Valley now known as Oregon City. Without a man, she was forced into servant status. One day Charles Dillingham, one of her employers, noticed her son playing with some yellow stones in a blue bucket. Astounded, Dillingham picked up a stone and discovered it was a nugget of pure gold. One of the "pebbles" was almost a pound of pure gold. All of the pebbles had been picked up by the boy on the banks of the dry creek bed where his mother had murdered his father.

The woman was understandably vague as to the location of the gold vein. Whoever found the gold would probably find her husband's body, and, although she undoubtedly looked upon the killing as justifiable homicide, she had no intention of standing trial for murder, no matter how much gold was involved. Her reticence probably also accounts for the many versions of the legend of the Blue Bucket gold or, as it more often is called erroneously, the Blue Bucket Mine. Only on her deathbed did the widow tell her son the location of the gold and her reason for keeping it secret. Thirty years, however, had dimmed her memory, and her son was more adept at practicing law than prospecting, so it is unknown whether or not he made even a cursory search for the treasure.

Another version of the lost Blue Bucket gold legend contends that T'Vault accompanied the Meek group. According to this account, all of the wagon masters lined up behind Meek in Fort Boise. Two of the trains pulled away from Meek, shortly after he embarked upon the "shortcut," returning to the Oregon Trail. Then, after the trail became nonexistent, the trains split into smaller units for more efficient movement. For a while Meek escorted a train commanded by a Captain Herren, but when this unit reached an area known as Wagontire Mountain, Meek went back to look for T'Vault, whose train was bringing up the rear. He found T'Vault, but was unable to find his way back to Wagontire. It was in T'Vault's wagon train, guided by Meek, that the murder of the alcoholic husband occurred and where the gold was scooped into a blue bucket by a small child.

This version is more explicit as to the probable location of the gold. It says that T'Vault threw Meek out of the train and sometime later brought his wagons to the fringe of a marshland now known as the Hart Mountain Antelope Range. Here they found a series of small holes containing stagnant but potable water. A camp was set up and scouts sent out to look for a way out of the mountains. Three days later one scout returned with a report of a better water hole some forty miles to the north. The train moved to the site. A new campground was established between two rises now known as Coyote Hills and Rabbit Hills. It was there that the blue bucket was filled with gold nuggets and the drunken husband was killed with a nail.

The motivation for the murder was stronger in this version. The little girl who died on the trail was the drunkard's daughter. He had beaten her so severely that she fell into a coma. She died about three days after the train moved on. She was buried on a hillside with an ox yoke and a toy cup to mark her grave. The drunkard's grave was marked by a wagon tailgate.

The search for the Blue Bucket gold has continued throughout the years. One of the more spectacular searches was organized in Portland in the summer of 1861. A man named Harold Adams spread the word around the Willamette Valley that he knew the location of the Blue Bucket gold. His boasts attracted the attention of a young man named Henry Griffin, an adventurer with a talent for organization.

Griffin made a deal with Adams that Adams would be paid $1,000 to lead a prospecting party to the site, and, if gold was discovered, he would be cut in for ten percent of the profits. Adams agreed.

Griffin made up a party of experienced prospectors, and in early August the well-equipped expedition set out from Portland under the guidance of Adams. The group wound a crooked trail through the Cascades, crossed the dry Oregon desert and, many days later, found itself in the area of the headwaters of the Burnt River. This was a spot considerably far from where Adams had indicated the Blue Bucket gold would be found.

That night, around the campfire, Griffin asked Adams for an explanation. "We're almost there," Adams replied.

"Will we be there tomorrow?" Griffin asked.

"Tomorrow or the next day."

"Will you stake your life on it?"

Adams did not answer. Later that night, however, after he thought all of his companions were asleep, he quietly saddled a horse. Before he could mount the animal, Griffin stopped him at gunpoint. The other prospectors were awakened. A unanimous vote approved the immediate "trial" of Adams, with Griffin acting as judge. It was probably one of the shortest trials in the history of the West. "You were running away because you have no idea where the Blue Bucket gold is," Griffin suggested.

Adams nodded his head.

The "jury," consisting of the other prospectors, then voted unanimously to strip Adams of all of his possessions except the clothes he wore and a canteen of water and to throw him out of the group.

Incredibly, the confidence man survived the long trek back across the desert. The following year, he was charged in Seattle with extortion for raising money to finance another expedition to find the Blue Bucket gold.

The prospecting party that had thrown him out in Oregon split into two segments the day after Adams's departure. The largest group turned toward the northwest and discovered what later became known as the rich John Day mines. The party, headed by Griffin, also is reported to have found gold in an area known as Elk Creek.

One of the most intensive expeditions in search of the lost Blue Bucket gold was a month-long foray financed by the late Erle Stanley Gardner shortly before his death. His search was based upon information furnished by Mrs. Lois Pierce of Hoodsport, Washington. She is descended from one of the families who took part in the historic Meek's Mistake.

According to journals in her possession, three persons in the wagon train died on consecutive days starting the day after a life-saving cloudburst. Her journals also indicate that the lost wagon train found water in what is now known as Lost Forest near Wagontire Mountain in central Oregon. Since a wagon train traveled about twelve miles a day, Gardner reasoned there should be three graves about twelve miles apart. He found a grave near a windmill on an abandoned ranch midway between Christmas Valley and Highway 395. About twelve miles away, another grave was discovered near Alkali Lake Station, and a third was located about another twelve miles south off Highway 395. Since the Gardner expedition worked backward, this placed the area of search between Rabbit Creek and Foley Creek, an area covered with potholed lava beds.

Gold often has been discovered under lava caps, most frequently in northern California, a short distance south of the

Gardner Expedition site. The gold originally was in streambeds that became conduits for lava spewed up by volcanic eruptions. Through continuing erosion over aeons, the streams once again wore away the lava, picked up the gold during cloudbursts, then deposited it in potholes as the stream again subsided.

Although Gardner failed to discover gold in the lava potholes between Rabbit and Foley creeks, there are many such lava beds in the area. If one finds the proper skeleton, he will have hit the nail on the head.

CACHIE'S CACHE

Cachie was an unfortunate Indian princess. She had the face of a burro, a deformed foot, and was as flat-chested as a table-top. Possibly to make up for these deficiencies, she was given more intelligence than many other Indians in her tribe. This only added to her difficulties, for if there was one thing an Indian warrior shunned more than a short, ugly woman, it was a squaw with brains. Not even the fact that she was the daughter of the Yavapai Indian Chief Quashackamo helped her lure a brave into her teepee. She was friendless and forlorn.

Whenever anyone did make a kind gesture in her direction, she became overwhelmed with gratitude. It is unknown what she did to repay kindly Indians. It is known, however, that on three separate occasions when she was befriended by a white person, she repaid the favor by divulging the location of a fortune. She was not believed on any of these three occasions. Two of the treasures later were found. The third is still undiscovered in Arizona.

Cachie was an only child, born in a teepee at some overnight camping site in the mid-1880s. Nothing is known of her mother, other than she died when Cachie was very young. If Cachie had not been an Indian princess, she probably would have been abandoned during her infancy because of her physical condition. By the time she reached puberty, she required a crude crutch to hobble around. She was an expert rider, however, and, because she was the daughter of a powerful Indian chief, she had her own pony, even though she was a girl.

When she was in her early teens, she was sent west by her father, Quashackamo. Apparently he was motivated by the dangerous political climate of Arizona in the late nineteenth century.

The commanding general of the army in the territory was the devious George Crook. Crook sought headlines in his war to exterminate the savages.

Massacres were not uncommon. After a group of whites raided an Indian concentration camp at Camp Grant and raped most of the women before slaughtering the entire community, Quashackamo decided that Arizona was, for the time being, no place for his crippled daughter. He sent her to live in a community of Chemehuevi Indians with whom the Yavapais had long enjoyed a friendly relationship.

The Chemehuevis, located near San Bernardino in California, accepted Cachie into their village, then ignored her. Cachie quickly learned to speak the dialect of the Chemehuevis, but even after she could communicate, she was ostracized. The Chemehuevis also had little use for an ugly squaw with brains, but Cachie did make friends with an elderly white couple who traded with the Indians. The two itinerant merchants operated out of San Bernardino, visiting several Indian villages in the area and trading knickknacks and baubles for moccasins and rugs, which they sold in their city store. Since there were no blood ties to hold the Indian princess to the Chemehuevis, one day she threw a blanket over her pony and followed the merchants to San Bernardino.

One of the other city merchants, an Englishman married to a Mexican woman, took Cachie into his home as a servant. Whether or not he realized that his guest was an Indian princess is unknown, but he certainly must have been impressed with the ease with which Cachie achieved fluency in English and Spanish. Within a few weeks, he had her working in his San Bernardino store as a clerk and interpreter. But it was a style of life that did not appeal to the princess.

It is unknown how long Cachie remained in San Bernardino or how she returned to Quashackamo, who then ruled his tribe from semipermanent headquarters on the banks of the Colorado River in Arizona. There are historical records, however, that refer to Quashackamo's daughter who sat at his side as an interpreter during meetings with Army men and merchants. Two of these accounts refer to Cachie's ugliness—one written by an emissary from General Crook who was trying to pressure Quashackamo into bringing his tribe into a reservation at Camp Date Creek, the other written in the diary of a miner named Charles Genung.

Genung was an enigma to his fellow white citizens in the territory. Both a prospector and a farmer, he was also a literate man in his early forties when he first met Cachie and her father. Although all the other white settlers were fighting the Indians, Genung preferred the company of Indians to whites. He lived by himself in a modest house in an area known as Peoples Valley, and apparently met Quashackamo during the time Cachie was in California. He met the Indian princess when she returned and became her father's interpreter. He described her as a "female of most ugly countenance to the point of fascination."

Genung's fascination with Cachie was not missed by the Indian princess. Anticipating that such interest probably would occur but once in her lifetime, she saddled her pony after one of Genung's visits and followed him back to Peoples Valley. Genung was not as forthright with his diary as could be desired. Although it is known that Cachie moved into Genung's modest home in Peoples Valley, there is some question as to whether she became his mistress or his housekeeper.

Cachie had been living with Genung for about a year when she decided to reward her benefactor. She told him the Yavapais knew of three locations where there was more gold than one man could spend in his lifetime. If Genung so wished, she would lead him to one of these locations. Genung smiled tolerantly and thanked her. Although he knew that Cachie was more intelligent than most Indian women, Genung had discovered that she also had a fertile imagination, and he did not want to embarrass her by accepting her offer.

Several months passed. Genung went on a prospecting foray and returned to Peoples Valley empty-handed. Again Cachie repeated her offer and when Genung again smiled, she drew him a map. "Go by yourself, then," she said quietly, passing him the paper.

Genung went to his small office, collected a gold nugget, a rock containing copper particles, and another filled with pyrites, sometimes known as fool's gold, then returned to Cachie. "One of these is gold," he said, placing the three specimens on the table. "Can you pick it out?"

Cachie instantly picked up the rock containing the shining copper particles. Genung patted her on the shoulder and carried his specimens back to his office. The next morning

Cachie was gone, and Genung heard a few days later that she was back with her father.

Five years later, gold was found in the Harquahalas Range in southwestern Arizona, resulting in the largest gold rush in Arizona's history. One mine alone in the area produced more than $15 million worth of gold before it was sold to an English syndicate for another $5 million. The Bonanza vein produced $4 million before it went dry, and the Golden Eagle vein adjacent to it was worth approximately $3 million.

When the gold rush was at its peak, Genung chanced across the map that Cachie had drawn for him earlier. The directions led him straight from Peoples Valley to the gold fields of the Harquahalas.

Cachie did not remain with her father very long. The U.S. Army was increasingly active in attempting to break up the Indian tribes. More white settlers were migrating into the fertile lands abutting the Colorado River. Quashackamo retreated deeper into the interior of the territory. Cachie, however, remained behind, moving in with a Mexican woman named Maria Valencia in the small mining town of La Paz.

Maria Valencia was an enormous woman with a husband who showed up about once a year. How Cachie and Maria became friendly is unknown, but it is known that Cachie also became friendly with the Ochoa family of La Paz through her relationship with Maria.

Long before the Harquahalas strike, Cachie attempted to give the Yavapais' secret away to Maria. Maria believed the story and she convinced her wandering husband upon one of his rare visits to La Paz to accompany Cachie to the site. Her husband, whose first name has long been forgotten, did accompany Cachie to the Harquahalas. Either Cachie did not show Valencia the gold fields, or Valencia could not recognize the

29

gold ore. He returned to La Paz several hours ahead of Cachie, told his wife and the Ochoas that the squaw was crazy, and outlined in detail the course and destination of his journey.

Maria died shortly after this foray, and Cachie disappeared. Three years later, when the gold strike was made in the Harquahalas, Peter Ochoa, a son of the people Cachie befriended, wryly recalled the scoffing comments made by Valencia about his trip into the mountains with the crazy Indian squaw.

When he was in his late teens, Peter Ochoa was given a job driving a freight wagon between Ehrenburg and Prescott, Arizona, along a route which took him through Peoples Valley. On one of these trips he met Genung and eventually discovered that they had a friend in common, Cachie. Ochoa learned also that Cachie, now forty years old and in poor health, had returned to Peoples Valley and was presently living in an abandoned miner's shack.

Ochoa stopped to see her. Quashackamo was dead. Cachie had no money and little to eat, but she still was an Indian princess—too proud to live on a reservation. Ochoa gave her a small supply of food and on his next trip a larger amount and some medical herbs prepared by his mother. During the late spring and the entire summer, Peter Ochoa never went through Peoples Valley without stopping to see Cachie to give her supplies and medicine.

One day in the early fall, Cachie hobbled out to his wagon as he was preparing to leave. "If you can come with two ponies, I will take you to a place where there is so much gold that you will never be able to spend it in your lifetime," she said.

"In the Harquahalas?"

Cachie nodded.

Ochoa stifled a sigh. "It has already been found, Cachie," he replied. "I thought you knew."

"Only on the north side. No one has found the gold on the south slope."

"How do you know?"

"My father showed me when I was a child."

Ochoa was convinced. Genung had told him of his experience with Cachie, and Ochoa had heard the words of Valencia. He promised to return within two weeks with the ponies.

It was closer to three weeks, however, before Ochoa was able to get back to Peoples Valley. There was no one in the shack that Cachie called her home. Peter Ochoa found her body under a tree about three hundred yards from her cabin.

For several years after Cachie's death, Ochoa searched the south slopes of the Harquahalas for the Yavapais' gold. He found several specimens of "rusty gold in quartz" at the bottom of arroyos, but he was never able to trace them to their source.

A story in the Yuma *Sentinel* in 1892 tells of two Frenchmen who deposited $8,000 worth of rusty, rough gold in the safe of the Hooper Company General Store and never returned to collect it. The description of the gold matches that found by Ochoa.

Another report of rusty gold in quartz is attributed to George Sears who, for many years, operated a small mine near Ajo, Arizona. En route from Ajo to Phoenix, he decided to do some prospecting. He made a detour into what he thought was the Eagle Tail Mountains, which are adjacent to the southern slope of the Harquahalas. In the side of a canyon, he found some loose rock that he thought worth assaying. He had loaded about twenty-five pounds of the ore on his mule when the skies suddenly darkened, then were split by lightning. Sears knew a canyon or a wash was no place to be during a mountain storm. Flash floods usually follow the downpour and to be caught in an arroyo means certain death. Sears hurriedly gathered up his tools, jumped on his horse, and galloped (leading his mule) down the canyon until he found a spot where he could climb up to a higher and safer elevation.

The storm was extraordinarily heavy and continued for several hours, leaving Sears and his animals thoroughly soaked. Below him, and between him and Phoenix, water raced down the canyon as forcefully as if it had escaped from a ruptured dam. Prudently, he decided to go back to Ajo and dry out. A day or so later he again set out for Phoenix, this time going there directly. An assayer confirmed that the ore he had picked up in the Eagle Tail Mountains did contain gold, lots of it.

Sears spent years looking for the lode. He was convinced that he knew where the canyon was, but he never could find it again. His only explanation was that the flash flood which followed the heavy storm had altered the terrain sufficiently to thwart recognition.

Today the Harquahalas are completely unpopulated. The booming town that arose coincidentally with the development of the mines is a ghostly accumulation of old foundations, crumbling fireplaces, and fragments of broken glass turned purple by the sun. Its post office, established in 1891, was discontinued in 1918, then revived from 1927 to 1932 under the name of Harqua. It has since vanished.

On most maps of the area there is a reference to the unbelievable Indian princess. Someone has named a water hole after her. It is known as Cachie's Tank.

HONEST HARRY MEIGGS

The North Beach section of San Francisco is an extension of the city's once infamous Barbary Coast. It is packed with night clubs, bars featuring topless and bottomless entertainment, cocktail lounges, restaurants with flamenco dancers and bull-fight movies, and Irish pubs where the darts fly in all directions. Buried or cached somewhere in this part of the city that is awake around the clock is $1 million worth of gold bullion stolen from the Bank of California by an alderman named Harry Meiggs. In all fairness to Honest Harry, however, he apparently was more concerned with making a name for himself than hustling a fast buck. He succeeded in the former endeavor but he was also fast with a dollar.

Honest Harry was born in New York, had an average school education in New England, and then was apprenticed as a hand in a lumberyard in Williamsburg, New York. He did not remain a hand very long, however, and there are conflicting stories as to how he wound up as proprietor of his own lumber-yard within two years. The most unkind theory suggests that Honest Harry simply stole enough lumber from his employer during the two years he worked for him to stock a competitive yard.

The life of a successful lumber merchant in Williamsburg soon palled for ebullient Harry, and, when word reached him of the gold strike in California, he decided to go west. He chartered a small ship, loaded it with the inventory in his yard and every other piece of lumber he could purchase on credit, and then filed for bankruptcy. It seemed pointless for him to wait around to answer embarrassing questions so, a few days after the petition for bankruptcy was filed, Harry sailed on his lumber-laden bark for San Francisco.

He could not have picked a better time to arrive in the "City by the Golden Gate." Although rich in gold and silver, San Francisco had no lumber to meet the building boom. Estimates of Honest Harry's profit on his cargo range from $50,000 to $500,000. The latter figure probably is more accurate in view of the fact that his New York creditors had met most of the initial cost.

Harry quickly decided there was more gold in lumber than there was in the Mother Lode country. He built a mill on North Beach, hired five hundred destitute miners, trained them to swing an axe, and launched the first assault upon California's redwood trees in the nearby canyons. A little more than two years after his arrival in the mid-1850s, the Mendocino mills of his California Lumber Company were supplying San Francisco with almost three million feet of redwood monthly.

If Harry had been content to remain a lumber baron, his name would long since have been forgotten. "I'm a lot bigger than a few planks of wood," he told a newspaper reporter immodestly. Harry raised funds to build the city's first opera house and sold them the lumber used in the construction. When a competitor raised funds to build the Jenny Lind Theatre, Harry exposed him as a swindler.

Harry ran for the city council and was elected. A few months later the city awarded the California Lumber Company a contract to build Meiggs Wharf, a monstrous pier that stretched from North Beach halfway to Alcatraz Island. A few days later, Honest Harry's lumber company won the first of several lucrative contracts to construct a road from Clarke's Point, around the face of Telegraph Hill, to North Beach. (The streets and roads at this time were constructed of heavy planking.)

It was a bank failure in the Panic of 1854 that started Honest Harry on his downfall. No one knows how much he lost, but it was enough so that he could not withstand the rising financial pressures of the depression. He was overextended on credit, and some reports claim that he was paying almost $250,000 annually as interest on loans. Harry, however, showed no visible signs of his problems. He still was considered a financial genius by his colleagues on the city council, and his offer to serve as chairman of the finance committee was gratefully accepted.

In this capacity it was easy to steal about a ream of "street warrants"—authorizations for payment by the city for the construction of roads and sidewalks. He filled out the forms for some $2 million worth of contracts to the California Lumber Company, then pledged them as security for loans from other banks in the city that had not folded.

No questions were raised. Honest Harry was the largest builder of streets and sidewalks in San Francisco, so it was natural that he should have such warrants tendered to him by the city. That Honest Harry sought the loans in gold bullion also was considered normal after Harry dropped the hint that he was involved in a large international financial transaction.

35

But when an observant bank clerk noticed that one of the warrants was payment for a sidewalk construction project that had been completed more than five years earlier, the matter was brought to the attention of the president of the bank, William C. Ralston.

A few nights later Ralston ran into Meiggs at a social function in the Occidental Hotel and cautioned him against holding the warrants for such a long period of time before cashing them. Honest Harry laughed off the advice, commenting that he had not needed the money, but the conversation was overheard by another alderman who became curious. He discovered the next day that the warrant for this construction project had been cashed two days after it was issued, and he thought it indeed strange that the same warrant could be used five years later as security for a loan. He went to Ralston who, in turn, called upon Meiggs.

"I don't understand it either," Honest Harry replied with a laugh. "I'll go through my books and let you know tomorrow."

Two hours later Honest Harry chartered the bark *America*, telling the captain to provision himself for a very long cruise and to plan for a midnight departure from the Broadway Wharf. During the afternoon Ralston and the suspicious alderman pored over the warrants hypothecated by Meiggs. Ralston checked with other bankers. By ten that evening, the banking community of San Francisco began to accept the truth: Honest Harry Meiggs, a pillar of the city, had indeed taken the city's leading bankers for almost $2 million in gold by pledging forged street warrants as security for loans.

Stopping only to pick up a deputy sheriff, the bankers sped by buggy to Meiggs's palatial home. A manservant in-

36

formed them that Meiggs had not yet returned from dinner. They waited.

The suspicious alderman, whose name has long been lost, meanwhile had driven to the offices of the California Lumber Company on North Beach. A heavy fog was rolling in from the Golden Gate and it put a chill in the air. The alderman said later that he did not know why he waited, but he did. Sometime around eleven, he spotted Honest Harry. Meiggs was coming out of the building carrying two canvas bank bags that appeared to be very heavy, a hammer, a saw, and a shovel. Honest Harry saw the alderman at the same time, shouted something unintelligible, then dove into a waiting cab. The driver whipped the horses and the hack disappeared in the fog, but not before the alderman got the cab number.

The cab driver returned to his base shortly after midnight to find the alderman and a policeman waiting. His story was short. Honest Harry had engaged him at the hack stand in front of the Occidental Hotel. They had gone directly to the California Lumber Company and upon leaving there had driven toward the Broadway Wharf. About halfway to their destination, Meiggs had told him to stop and again wait. He then disappeared in the fog, carrying both canvas bags and his tools. He returned in about twenty minutes carrying the tools and one canvas bag. They then went to the Broadway Wharf, where Honest Harry left him with the tools and a five-dollar tip.

About an hour after midnight, Ralston, other bilked bankers, the alderman, the deputy sheriff, the police officer, and a reporter from *The Alta*, were clustered on the Broadway Wharf. Despite the dense fog and the lack of a breeze, the bark *America* had cast off shortly after midnight. Although no one had seen Honest Harry board the vessel, it was the only ship to have sailed since he had arrived at the wharf. Therefore, it was reasonable to presume, the pursuers decided, that Meiggs was on board the *America*.

The only wrath greater than that of a woman scorned is that of a mulcted banker. On the Broadway Wharf were five of the city's leading bankers and every one was in a fury. They knew Meiggs was escaping with $2 million worth of their gold, and they wanted him caught, no matter what the cost.

At the end of the wharf was the small coastal steamer *The Active*. The bankers, the police, and the reporter descended upon the boat en masse. The captain of *The Active* was reluctant to sail. It would take an hour to get up steam, and the fog was so dense that it would be impossible to find the bark. The bankers waved money, so the skipper decided to try the impossible. In little less than an hour, *The Active* cast off, headed full steam in the general direction of the Golden Gate, and promptly rammed into the side of a coal barge.

With the dawn coming, a slight breeze sprang up. It blew away the fog and the bankers found they had drifted to a point about a mile east of Alcatraz Island. Less than three hundred yards off their starboard bow, which still was impaled on the coal barge, was the bark *America*. The same breeze that blew away the fog puffed the sails of the bark. Leaning over the taffrail as the *America* swept toward the Golden Gate was Honest Harry Meiggs.

Ralston was convinced that Honest Harry had only taken half of his gold with him. The hack driver identified the canvas bags carried by Meiggs as similar to those the bank used for transporting coin and bullion. He repeated his story: that

38

Honest Harry had left his office with two heavy canvas bags, that he had stopped about midway between the office and the wharf where he had mysteriously disposed of one of the bags. A small clump of moist dirt remained on the shovel that was left in the hack. Weeks were spent searching for some signs of hasty digging in the area, but nothing was found.

Honest Harry did not disappear. From Hawaii he wrote letters to acquaintances, and this so infuriated Ralston that he prevailed upon Governor John Bigler to start extradition proceedings. By the time the papers arrived in Hawaii, however, Honest Harry had moved on.

He next appeared in Chile where he immediately began to operate in much the same manner as he had in San Francisco. Here, with the help of government officials as silent partners, he built railroads instead of planked streets. According to one published report he realized a $1,300,000 profit on a 33-mile stretch of track laid between Valparaiso and Santiago. He built a large castle, which he named La Quinta, for his home. On one occasion he put it up as the grand prize in a charitable lottery, but Honest Harry's "luck" still held for he had purchased the winning ticket.

The unforgiving Ralston continued to labor for Meiggs's extradition, as Honest Harry still made no secret of his whereabouts. Extradition papers sent to Chile disappeared. Ralston went to Governor Bigler and then wrote to Washington. A short time later, Bigler was appointed to the position of American Minister to Chile. He personally carried Honest Harry's extradition papers with him. A short time after his arrival in Chile, Bigler personally quashed the extradition. Meiggs wrote to friends in San Francisco that he still planned to return "to pick up some investments."

A change of administration in Chile sent Honest Harry

Meiggs north to Peru where he remained for the next decade and where he left a name that never will be forgotten in South America. It was Meiggs who promoted the construction of the Trans-Andean railroad, described as one of the awful tragedies of history. More than ten thousand lives were lost in its construction and its $200-million cost virtually bankrupted the Peruvian government. Much of this passed through Meiggs's wallet, but, like many confidence men, Honest Harry spent his money as soon as he touched it. At his hacienda near Callao, he hosted parties that cost more than $200,000. Usually, a few days after a party a contract for another segment of the useless railroad would be let to Meiggs and his silent partners in the government.

The end of the Peruvian venture came in the mid-1870s. The government could borrow no more capital to finance rail construction and soon could not raise enough money internally to meet the interest payments on money borrowed earlier. The railroad remained unfinished.

"I am planning to return to San Francisco," Honest Harry wrote to an acquaintance there. "I have a million-dollar investment in the city, and, if certain formalities are undertaken successfully, I plan to spend the waning years of my life there quietly."

The "formalities" soon became evident. A special bill was introduced in the California assembly which would grant amnesty to Meiggs should he return. It was passed and then referred to the California senate where it also was quietly passed, but not so quietly that word of the maneuvering did not reach Ralston.

The banker rushed to the state capital and prevailed upon the governor to veto it. Honest Harry's influence apparently was well financed, for both the assembly and the senate promptly overrode the veto. Ralston then reached the state attorney general who announced that the bill was unconstitutional and that he would carry the matter to the state supreme court. Once the issue had attracted the attention of the newspapers, the lawmakers promptly lost interest in the future plans of Honest Harry Meiggs.

Shortly after news of this defeat reached Meiggs in Peru, he was seized by apoplexy. He lived for only a short time afterward in a state of paralysis, and died on September 29, 1877, at the age of sixty-six in his Callao hacienda.

Soon after Meiggs died, Ralston committed suicide when his Bank of California collapsed.

Somewhere in the North Beach there surely is hidden $1 million worth of gold bullion, stolen by Honest Harry Meiggs from Ralston's Bank of California. It lies somewhere along the old road that led from the offices of the California Lumber Company to the Broadway Wharf. Perhaps it could be found with a metal detector, but the treasure seeker would have to put up with such distractions as nude or flamenco dancers, dart-throwing gamesters, bullfight *aficionados*, or someone simply enjoying a good steak. But it might be a good escape for the treasure seeker who is tired of the desert and the sea.

THE SINKING
OF THE
"ADA HANCOCK"

At approximately five o'clock on the afternoon of April 27, 1863, a small ferry steamer named the *Ada Hancock* blew up midway between the Banning Dock in Wilmington and Dead Man's Island in Los Angeles Harbor. Twenty-six of the fifty-six persons on board were known to have been killed.

Investigators, probing in the primitive manner of the times, were unable to reach a conclusion as to the cause of the explosion. The vessel was carrying several barrels of gun powder loaded from a coastal freighter earlier in the day, but not yet placed ashore. One employee of the company which owned the ship reported that the boiler was defective. Not much attention was paid to his testimony, however, because not only was he a Mexican, but he had been fired the morning of the accident because of a knee injury that slowed him down on the job.

There were a few potential murder victims aboard the *Ada Hancock* who were killed in the accident. One was a businessman whose life had been threatened by a competitor. Another was a Southern Californian who was trying to get rid of a clinging mistress. A third was a doctor who was running off with another man's wife. A small-time robber baron was blown from the deck of the steamer and, according to one report, "landed ashore on his feet escaping injury." This qualifies as a miraculous escape indeed as the *Ada Hancock* was about a mile from shore when it blew up. One of the most intriguing solutions to the sinking of the *Ada Hancock* did not appear until a half-century after the explosion, long after the tragedy was forgotten by most people. This solution, which is the most probable, not only accounts for the explosion, but also for the disappearance of more than $125,000 of Wells Fargo gold.

When it exploded, the *Ada Hancock* was ferrying passengers from the dock to the S.S. *Senator*, a coastal steamer anchored at Dead Man's Island, scheduled for an early evening departure to San Francisco. At this time there were but two piers in Los Angeles Harbor. One was the Banning Dock owned by Phineas Banning in the town of Wilmington, a community that Banning ran like a fiefdom. The other was owned by a man named Timms and was located in the adjacent and somewhat larger town of San Pedro. Neither the docks nor the harbor entrance were large enough to accommodate the deep draft of a coastal steamer the size of the *Senator*.

The only communication between these waterfront towns and Los Angeles, other than by messenger, was by telegraph wire with terminals in San Pedro and Camp Drumm. The latter was a small military outpost in Wilmington that had achieved fame of a sort for being the headquarters of the military's ill-fated camel corps.

Shortly before four o'clock, about one hour before the

Ada Hancock cast off, someone cut the telegraph wire at about the midway point between San Pedro and Los Angeles. As a result, more than five hours passed before news of the *Ada Hancock* tragedy reached Los Angeles, less than twenty miles away.

The seasonal high fog and clouds hung over the harbor, and there was a slight chill in the air. Most of the passengers already on board the *Senator* were either in their cabins or in the salon when the *Ada Hancock* left the Banning Dock for the last time. One of the exceptions was a Dr. Paul Henry who was on the deck of the coastal steamer.

"The ferry started to cast off, then was made fast again to allow a man to board," he reported. "Then it backed away from the dock, made its turn, and proceeded toward me. I watched it for a short period of time, then stepped back to make way for one of the crew. It was then that I heard the gunfire. I looked back just in time to see the explosion. The *Ada Hancock* simply disintegrated. Bodies and debris from the vessel rose into the air, appearing to move very slowly. After the explosion, the only sound I heard immediately was a long piercing shriek of a woman. The vessel had disappeared. Then the bodies and flotsam fell back into the water. A huge bubble of air escaped from the bottom of the harbor. A moment later a large wave, created by the explosion, rocked the *Senator*. It was after this that I became aware of the faint cries for help, and that I realized that incredibly there were some survivors of this disaster."

Dr. Henry reported at once to the captain of the *Senator*, and the main salon of the ship was prepared as an infirmary while the lifeboats were lowered to pick up the survivors. There is no record as to how many of the survivors were taken to the *Senator*. The coastal steamer sailed that night for San

Francisco carrying its injured with it. Dr. Henry's version of the explosion was given to San Francisco reporters upon the ship's arrival there. It is known only that there were fifty-six people on board the *Ada Hancock* when it exploded and that there were twenty-six known fatalities.

One of the survivors taken to San Francisco was Edgar Smith. He told reporters that there was a gun battle below deck immediately preceding the explosion.

Those survivors missed by the lifeboats of the *Senator* were not so fortunate. Because telegraphic communication with Los Angeles was severed, only the staff medical officer from nearby Camp Drumm was available to treat the injured. Most were transported by wagon for treatment at the military base.

All agreed that there had been gunfire immediately before the explosion, but those who had been on the top deck said the shots came from below. Conversely, those who were on the lower deck insisted the gunfire erupted on the top deck. Some contended that the vessel's boiler blew up. Others reported the heavy smell of gunpowder right after the blast.

Many bodies washed ashore during the evening. Most were promptly stripped and looted, then buried, either by soldiers from Camp Drumm or by waterfront derelicts.

The day after the explosion word of the disaster's extent reached Los Angeles. Among those seriously concerned were officials of the local branch of the Wells Fargo Bank, because one of the passengers scheduled to sail on the *Senator* had been a Wells Fargo messenger named William Ritchie. The messenger was carrying $25,000 in gold destined for the San Francisco Mint.

An official of the bank was dispatched to Wilmington where he learned that Ritchie had indeed been on the last voyage of the *Ada Hancock*. It was not known whether or not he was one of the survivors taken on board the *Senator*. More than a century ago, bank auditors were as suspicious of disappearing employes as they are today. An audit was taken of the bank's resources. The $25,000, as expected, had been picked up by Ritchie on the previous day. What was unexpected, however, was the disappearance of an additional $100,000 worth of gold bullion. In fact, the gold reserves of the Wells Fargo office in Los Angeles had been wiped out.

The investigation quickly disclosed that the authorized shipment of gold had been taken out of the bank by Ritchie a little past noon on the preceding day. Shortly before this he had been seen with Louis Scheslinger, another Wells Fargo messenger who, as a sideline, dabbled in usurious loans. Word was put out immediately for Scheslinger to come to the bank, but to no avail. He had disappeared as completely as Ritchie.

Louis Scheslinger had arrived in Los Angeles from his native New York when he was in his late teens. A big, powerful youth with a quick mind, he easily secured a job with Wells Fargo as a guard. Within a few months he was promoted to messenger and soon thereafter was entrusted with carrying large shipments of gold and currency between Los Angeles and San Francisco.

He also demonstrated a talent for making money. Within weeks after his arrival he was making loans to small Mexican landholders who did not qualify for a loan from the bank and who were sufficiently in need of funds to be willing to pay an exhorbitant interest. He usually foreclosed on the landowner the day after the note became due and sold the property quickly for a substantial profit. He was not the only loan shark operating in Southern California during this period, but most of the others were willing to wait until the crops were harvested before they collected their money. The idea of foreclosure was foreign to the Mexicans and to the community, so Scheslinger's habit did not make him a popular man in Los Angeles. It was unlikely that Scheslinger cared about his popularity for, by the summer of 1862, he had acquired sufficient capital to lend $30,000 to a Don Ricardo Vejar, who used his huge ranch east of Los Angeles as collateral. The interest charged on the loan is not known. It is known, however, that the loan was for one year's duration, and there was a clause in the loan agreement stating that the full amount would become due immediately in the event of Don Ricardo's death. On April 20, 1863, one week before the *Ada Hancock* blew up, Don Ricardo Vejar was injured fatally when he was thrown from a stallion on his ranch.

Scheslinger heard of the accident on the following day. He immediately had foreclosure papers drawn up and, accompanied by one Hyman Tishell and another unidentified man, arrived at the Vejar hacienda in late afternoon with his ultimatum: Pay me or I'll take the ranch.

Ramon Vejar, the eldest son of Don Ricardo, was not sympathetic to Scheslinger's claim. The body of Don Ricardo was not yet buried. There were members of the family who had not arrived for the funeral. At first he reacted as if Scheslinger were perpetrating a bad joke, but when he became convinced that the loan shark was indeed serious, he became very calm, picked up the papers Scheslinger had brought with him, asked the loan shark to wait for his return, then left the room.

Tishell described the scene later. "When we arrived there were all the usual sounds that one expects on a busy ranch. But shortly after Ramon Vejar left the room, it slowly became quiet outside. Soon, I could only hear the sound of the wind. I went to the window and looked out. The Mexicans and all of the animals had disappeared except for our horses. I told Louis we ought to get out of there."

Despite the pleas and suggestions from his companions, Scheslinger did not want to leave. Ramon Vejar had disappeared with the foreclosure papers and if Scheslinger left without them, he would be forced to make another trip from Los Angeles. Approximately three-quarters of an hour after Vejar left, Schlesinger went out of the room and searched for his inhospitable host through several other rooms on the ground floor of the hacienda. There was not a sign of a human being or animal. He called out Vejar's name. There was no answer. The building had been abandoned. He returned to the room where Tishell waited with his friend and now their uneasiness infected him. It took very little urging from Tishell to get him to agree to leave.

The trio waited by the open door a long time. The outside seemed emptier and more ominous than the deserted hacienda. Even the dogs and the chickens had disappeared. The corral was empty. The only signs of life were the three horses on which they had arrived. Still saddled, the horses remained tied to a hitching post near the main entrance to the building. Unsheathing their revolvers, the three men walked across the open patio to their mounts.

About a half-hour later, the three men breathed a collective sigh of relief as they slowed their horses from a gallop to a canter and replaced their guns in their holsters. Although they were still on the Vejar ranch, they were now out of sight of the silent hacienda.

"Louis was becoming very angry," Tishell reported. "He said he was going to come back with a posse and throw out the Vejars so hard they would bounce all the way back to Mexico."

A moment later the three men were ambushed. They had

just entered a small arroyo. The unidentified member of the trio was in front, with Tishell and Scheslinger following in that order. They never saw their attackers, who were lying on the ground concealed by rocks and boulders. Only one volley of shots was fired, but it instantly killed the unidentified man and his horse. Two bullets struck Tishell, but he managed to remain on his horse and race through the arroyo to safety. Scheslinger wheeled his horse around, fled out of the arroyo in the direction from which he had come, and escaped unscathed. He took a circuitous route back to Los Angeles, catching up with the wounded Tishell near the San Gabriel Mission. Tishell was left at the mission for treatment of his wounds and returned to Los Angeles the following day.

It was a badly frightened loan shark who reported the ambush and killing to the Los Angeles sheriff later that evening. The sheriff's reaction to the incident is unknown, but apparently he was not very sympathetic to Scheslinger's cause as there is no record of his undertaking any punitive action against Ramon Vejar.

Investigators for the Wells Fargo Bank pieced together Scheslinger's movements. The day after the ambush Scheslinger began to sell off his mortgages, discounting some as much as fifty percent. He visited the wounded Tishell. "He was in mortal fear of the Mexican, Vejar," Tishell reported. "Vejar was half his size, but he [Scheslinger] was afraid of him. He offered to sell me the Vejar mortgage for five thousand dollars, but I refused. If Louis couldn't collect on it, how could I?"

Scheslinger did sell the Vejar mortgage, however, along with several others to a man named Clark who paid for them with cash drawn from a Wells Fargo account. On the morning of April 27, Scheslinger appeared at the bank shortly after it opened and withdrew his account in cash. The amount of money in his possession at this time is unknown, but the most conservative estimate would place it at several thousand dollars.

Late in the forenoon, Scheslinger was seen talking to William Ritchie in the lobby of the Bella Union Hotel. In the early afternoon he was again seen with Ritchie outside the Wells Fargo Bank just before Ritchie picked up the gold shipment that he was scheduled to take to San Francisco. Bank investigators in Los Angeles could not find anyone who had seen Scheslinger after this.

The bank detectives discovered that three metal boxes bearing Wells Fargo seals were carried by Ritchie on the stage to Wilmington. One of these boxes was more than sufficient to hold the legitimate shipment. The investigators went to Wilmington and learned that Ritchie had carried three bank boxes on board the *Ada Hancock*.

In the course of their investigation, the detectives ran across the Mexican deckhand who had been fired from his job on the *Ada Hancock* because of his knee injury. He told an intriguing story. He had been at the dock while the *Ada Hancock* was preparing for her final voyage. The stern lines had been cast off and the vessel was swinging away from the dock when Louis Scheslinger ran up demanding that he be taken on board. A crewman tossed the line back to a workman on the dock who fastened it around a bit. The crew then pulled the vessel back to the pier.

"He was very, very angry," the deckhand said, adding that he knew Scheslinger well because of his many trips to San Francisco.

There were several witnesses to confirm that there had been a late boarder, but other than the injured deckhand, none could identify him. Late boardings were not uncommon since tickets could be purchased on the vessel. The detectives learned that Scheslinger had not traveled to Wilmington by stage. He was known to the drivers, and none had seen him.

Three days after the explosion Ritchie's body washed ashore near Timms' Landing. It was so badly mangled that identification could be made only from clothes remnants and an ornate gun holster that Ritchie favored. The holster was empty.

Here is where the investigation conducted by the Wells Fargo detectives ended. In the final report on the case, it was deduced that Ritchie may have been trying to double-cross his partner, Scheslinger, in the bank theft and had been caught at the last minute. The gun battle on board the *Ada Hancock*, which immediately preceded the explosion, may well have been carried out by these two men. The report adds that the answer will probably never be known as there is nothing besides the statement of a disgruntled Mexican to indicate that Scheslinger was on board. The report did conclude, however, that the stolen gold was on board the *Ada Hancock* when she blew up.

By 1912 the activity around Los Angeles Harbor was much greater than in the days when Banning and Timms competed for the wharfage business. In the summer of that year, workmen excavating for footings for a new building unearthed a shallow grave. It contained the skeleton of a large young man in his late twenties. In the middle of his skull was a bullet hole. The only clue to his identity was a tarnished belt buckle lying near the bones. Inscribed upon the buckle were the initials L.S.

The location of the grave was not far from the old

Banning Dock. Detectives did not pursue their investigation of this apparent murder with vigor because the coroner's office placed the time of death about a half-century earlier.

It is not unreasonable to assume that in the remains of the *Ada Hancock* lies more than $125,000 in gold. Dead Man's Island has disappeared, long since dredged away, but its location still is known. Also long gone is Banning's Dock, but its former location also is known. In a straight line between the two points, about a mile off shore lies what is left of the *Ada Hancock*.

THE VASQUEZ INGOT

About an hour's drive north of Los Angeles is the Vasquez Rocks Recreation Area. These pockmarked rocks, thrust up to heights in excess of two hundred feet by temblors along the San Andreas Fault, sprawl over a large area near the southern end of the Mojave Desert. The Vasquez Rocks area is a familiar sight to countless Western Americana buffs, as they provide one of Hollywood's favorite location sites for motion picture and television Westerns. These rocks, clustered over more than a thousand acres, are as full of holes as a piece of wormwood. In all probability there is a 500-pound ingot of pure silver that was hidden in one of these holes by a rather prominent California bandit of a century ago named Tiburcio Vasquez.

The huge ingot was cast as a precaution against a planned hijack from a silver mine several miles from the town of Panamint. Panamint was one of the more violent mining camps of the era. The first man to discover silver in the area, William Alvord, was murdered by a berserk partner before an ounce of ore was processed. Mining started on a minor scale in 1861 and remained small for almost a decade because of the inaccessibility of the community. The town was located at the head of a canyon more than a mile deep in the mountains adjacent to Death Valley. For more than a decade after the first silver strike, the only way into Panamint was over a steep trail not wide enough in some areas for two horses to pass.

Many of the mining claims were worked by outlaws. One story claims that since so much of Panamint's population was wanted by the law elsewhere, postmasters automatically forwarded mail addressed to known desperados there for delivery. Another tells of two highwaymen who sought refuge in Panamint after holding up a Wells Fargo stage. The pair struck a rich silver lode, sold out for $25,000 and went to San Francisco to collect their money. Here they were recognized. The loot from the stage robbery had been approximately $5,000, but the bank manager gave the two outlaws an out. If they paid the bank one hundred percent interest on the "loan," Wells Fargo would not prosecute them. The two former bandits sold their $25,000 check for $15,000 and departed.

Around 1869 Robert L. Stewart, with two partners, found an exceptionally rich lode in the mountains above Panamint. Unlike most of their fellow miners, these men were well financed. They brought in cheap Chinese labor from San Francisco, built a rough road down the side of the mountain and a small smelter. The smelter not only processed the ore of their own Wonder Mine, but that of some of the small mines in the area.

Early in the summer of 1872, Senator William M. Stewart of Nevada strayed from his constituency to visit his brother Robert in Panamint. Stewart had made a fortune in the famed Comstock Lode in Nevada. He was a miner and a gambler with a fondness for cards, and so, when he paused in Neagle's

Occidental Saloon and saw a game of faro in progress, he promptly invited himself to participate. Among the players were John Small and John McDonald, two men of dubious reputation, who operated a small mine near the Wonder Mine.

McDonald and Small were surly men, liked only by each other. They were poor card players, also, but were tolerated in the games because they consistently lost. Usually after they had lost all of the silver in their possession, they would skulk back to their mine, which they ran with cheap Chinese labor.

The witty and gregarious senator was the exact opposite of the poor miners and, possibly because of this, they made known their dislike for the politician immediately. Apparently Senator Stewart was thick-skinned, and he ignored the thinly disguised insults tossed in his direction by Small and McDonald. He finally reacted, however, by raising the stakes in the game. Either the senator was extraordinarily lucky or exceptionally skilled in the game because within a half-hour, Stewart had bankrupted the game.

The two miners were furious. They did not dare to accuse Stewart of cheating, but they did question the senator's lucky streak.

"It is bound to turn," Stewart replied amiably. "It is unfortunate that neither of you gentlemen any longer have the funds to take advantage of this turn."

McDonald reacted angrily. "I'll put up five percent of our mine against the five thousand you have won here tonight in one game of showdown."

"I know nothing about your mine," Stewart replied, "but I will accept your wager."

A patron of the saloon was pressed into service as a dealer. Showdown is a game in which five cards are dealt from a deck in turn, and the winner is the man with the best poker hand. Neither McDonald nor Stewart touched the cards. When the last card was dealt, McDonald was the winner with a pair of kings. He reached for the money, then paused as Stewart held up his hand. "Once again," the senator said. "Ten thousand cash against ten percent of your mine."

McDonald hesitated, then nodded. Again the cards were dealt and again he won. Stewart raised his bet again, this time to $15,000, and when this hand was lost, he doubled his bet again. McDonald was dealt a full house over Stewart's pair of kings. The senator now owed the miner $60,000. The drinking and the other games in the saloon had stopped; the players and the patrons crowded around the small, round table with the green-felt top. Stewart was calm. Both McDonald and Small were flushed with elation.

"You value your mine at one hundred thousand dollars," Stewart said. "I will double the bet once more for one hundred and twenty thousand against the entire mine."

This time McDonald nodded with no hesitation.

"I must remind you that I am due for a win," Stewart said calmly.

"Deal," McDonald replied.

The winning hand has never been forgotten in Panamint. The first two cards dealt to McDonald were queens. The last three cards dealt to the senator from Nevada were aces. For a long time the cards remained on the table where they had fallen. Then McDonald swept them to the floor with the back of his hand. "Show me the money you would have paid me if you had lost," he demanded.

The onlookers sighed collectively. Senator Stewart nodded, took out his wallet and extracted a blank check. He asked for a pen, and one was brought from the bar. He then proceeded to make out a check to cash in the amount of $120,000.

With a flourish, he showed it first to the dealer, then to Mc-
Donald and Small. Then he tore the check into pieces and
dropped them on the table. "It's not safe to carry this much
money around in cash," he said.

"How do we know it would have been good?" Small
asked. This remark was nearly as dangerous as an accusation
of cheating, but the senator brushed it off. "I didn't question
your ownership of a mine," he replied, "and how many years
will it take me to collect your debt from the ground?"

Small and McDonald remained in Panamint, angry and
moody. Stewart was shown his newly acquired holdings on
the following day by other residents of the town and he
immediately ensured the loyalty of his Chinese employees by
dividing $1,000 among them as a bonus.

For several weeks, Stewart remained in the area, com-
muting between a boardinghouse in Panamint and the mine.
The two former owners ventured out of the community to
prospect occasionally, but for most of the time they sulked
in one of the saloons. At first they complained bitterly about
their ill fortune. Then their complaints took another tack.
They claimed they had been swindled out of their mine by
a crooked politician. When this was followed by muttered
threats of revenge, McDonald and Small were paid a visit by
the sheriff.

"If anything happens to Senator Stewart, I won't have
to go far to find a couple of men for the hanging tree," the
lawman warned.

A short time later, a Mexican card dealer arrived at the
mine to see Stewart. On the previous evening, he told the
senator, he had been approached by McDonald and offered
a share in the proceeds if he would participate in the robbery
of Stewart's first shipment of silver to Los Angeles. A Mexican

was needed as a front man, the dealer explained, so that the robbery would be attributed to the bandit Tiburcio Vasquez. The dealer added with remarkable candor that he had refused only because he distrusted both Small and McDonald. Both of the former owners had indicated they would go ahead with the robbery, with or without the Mexican's help.

Stewart had been planning to send out his first shipment on the following day on a couple of pack mules, but because of this warning he changed his mind.

Small and McDonald gave no indications of abandoning their plans as the days turned into weeks and the amount of silver increased with each day's production. After nearly two months had elapsed, Stewart received some more disquieting news from informers in Panamint. Small and McDonald were becoming impatient and were making plans to raid the mine.

Stewart was in a quandary. He and his brother had made arrangements to sell both mines to a conglomerate in Los Angeles. The prospective purchasers were somewhat worried over Panamint's reputation for violence. Both Stewarts had assured the purchaser that such reports were grossly exaggerated. A raid on the mine could defeat the sale. The posting of armed guards might have a similar effect.

No gangs or bands were involved. The senator had five Chinese workers on his payroll, none of whom would back him up in a gunfight. Small and McDonald were unpopular in Panamint and so were unlikely to attract a following in the raid. As soon as he had realized this, Senator Stewart came up with an idea.

His ore had been refined crudely at his brother's smelter, then returned daily to the senator's mine for storage. At that time, he had approximately one thousand pounds of silver in his possession. In a shed near the mine Stewart built a furnace. Then he had his employees build a large mold. The silver was remelted, poured inside the mold and allowed to harden. When the project was concluded, Stewart had two huge ingots, each weighing approximately five hundred pounds.

A few days after this, the Mexican card dealer visited Stewart in the Panamint boardinghouse. He told the senator that Small and McDonald were planning to raid the mine the following day, take all the silver they could carry on two pack mules, and carry it all the way to San Francisco. Stewart smiled quietly and asked his Mexican friend to join him in witnessing the raid. Before sunrise the two men, each carrying a pair of powerful binoculars, were ensconced on a steep hill overlooking the mine.

Small and McDonald arrived at the mine around 9:00 A.M. Each was on horseback and each was leading a pack mule. The Chinese, squatting silently near the mine shaft, offered no resistance to the armed men. The foreman cooperated by telling the miners that the senator had not arrived today and by showing them the shed where the huge ingots were stored. The instant Small and McDonald entered the shed, the Chinese workers disappeared, scrambling up the side of the hill to hide behind rocks. A moment later loud curses rang out from the shed. The foreman burst out of the door and also fled into the hills. He too was out of sight before the two miners came out into the open again. Still swearing loudly, they rigged a sling from some rope they had brought with them and used the mules to drag the heavy ingots out from the shed. Then both struggled to lift the ingot in its sling to the back of the mule, but they were small men and the weight was too much for them. For more than two hours they wrestled with the huge bars before they became convinced that they were too heavy for them to hoist. Then they spent another hour or so rigging up an A-frame with a pully. Stewart became slightly worried when the men raised one of the ingots to the apex of the frame, but as McDonald led a mule underneath it, one of the legs of the frame collapsed. The frame fell, striking the mule who bolted and followed the Chinese miners up the hill.

In mid-afternoon the two men gave up. They had twice rebuilt the A-frame. It had collapsed once. The second time, when they lowered the quarter-ton silver ingot to the back of the mule, the animal sank to the ground, unable to stand. Small and McDonald were too exhausted to swear anymore. They mounted their horses and departed. They were never seen in Panamint again.

"How are you going to get such a large piece of silver to Los Angeles, señor?" the card dealer asked Stewart after Small and McDonald had disappeared.

"I guess I'll have to use Remi Nadeau," Stewart replied.

Nadeau was known as the boss teamster of California. His twenty-mule freight teams with their blue wagons roamed all over the southern part of the state hauling everything from ore to borax. Unknown to Stewart was the fact that Nadeau, along with several of his muleskinners, maintained a very friendly relationship with the bandit Tiburcio Vasquez. Their friendship had started a few years earlier on a day when Nadeau was driving in his buggy to one of his desert way-stations. Earlier that day Vasquez had been shot during a stagecoach holdup attempt, was assumed dead, and was left on the desert trail. When Nadeau came upon Vasquez, the bandit was still alive. Nadeau carried him in the buggy to his nearest freight station where he told the keeper to hide Vasquez and nurse him back to health.

Vasquez repaid the kind deed by ordering that none of

his followers ever hold up a Nadeau freight team, a reaction
the wily teamster boss might possibly have foreseen when he
played the Good Samaritan role. The bandit kept his word.
On several occasions his band of outlaws were seen swooping
down on a Nadeau freight train, only to veer off when the
distinctive blue wagons were recognized.

There was one exception however. This was on the day
that Nadeau sent a buckboard to Stewart's mine to pick up the
two 500-pound ingots.

The buckboard was driven by a man named James Funk.
He loaded the ingots with no problem and hauled them into
Panamint where, a short time later, they were transferred to
one of Nadeau's freight wagons for the long haul into Los
Angeles. For no apparent reason the buckboard was fastened
to the rear of the freight wagon and was towed along when
the train left Panamint. Also going along on the trip was teamster Funk.

Tiburcio Vasquez and his band struck the freight train
near the rocks which bear his name and where he often sought
refuge. With the band was a harnessed mule, which was
quickly hitched to the buckboard. Other members of the band
wrestled one of the ingots from the freighter to the buckboard.
The other 500-pound bar of silver bullion was left on the
train. Nothing else was taken. The buckboard and the band
of outlaws headed for Vasquez Rocks; the freight wagon
started once again for Los Angeles.

It was not until the following day that a posse reached
Vasquez Rocks, and the buckboard was found abandoned.
There was no sign of Vasquez or his band.

Funk and the mule skinners were shown pictures of
Vasquez and all identified him as the leader of the gang
which had held up the freighter.

Three weeks later Vasquez and three members of his gang appeared at the ranch of Alessandro Repetto, nine miles from Los Angeles in what is now Hollywood. Repetto was not happy to see the outlaws. On their last visit they had stolen a mule from him and had threatened to kill him if he reported it. This time Vasquez wanted eight hundred dollars.

"I don't have it," Repetto protested.

"Then write a check," Vasquez demanded.

Repetto did as he was asked, and a boy who worked for him was sent to the bank in Los Angeles to cash it. Some time after the youth had left the bank to return to the ranch, the banker became suspicious of the transaction and notified the sheriff. The sheriff sent a deputy to the ranch. Vasquez and his companions had left, but when Repetto identified the extortionist as the notorious bandit, the deputy quickly rounded up a posse to give chase.

Vasquez was trailed to an area known as Tujunga Pass and then back to Hollywood where, a few days later, he was wounded and captured in a vacant ranch house. When he recovered, he was taken to San Jose and charged with murder in connection with the death of two persons during a stage holdup. Shortly before he was hanged, he was visited in the San Jose jail by Stewart.

"What happened to my silver ingot?" the senator asked the outlaw.

Vasquez shrugged. "It's in a hole in the rocks," he replied. He would tell Stewart nothing more.

The bandit also had another visitor, Remi Nadeau, a few hours before his execution. "I thought we had an arrangement," Nadeau said.

Vasquez spread out his palms. "There was a problem," he said. "I have a cousin who is a card dealer in Panamint, and it was he who told me of the shipment. I had an obligation to him. But I also am your friend, Remito. I owe you my life. This is why I only took one of the ingots. Do you understand?"

Nadeau was not sure that he did.

There are many holes in Vasquez Rocks. The huge silver ingot will be as tarnished as the rocks in which it lies hidden. The area is easy to get to—a paved road leads right into it. There are even facilities for overnight camping.

THE VEKOL INVESTMENT

John D. Walker had always been considered a little odd by those who knew him. He came to Arizona in the mid-1860s when the Indians were believed to be such a menace that they required extermination by the United States Army. Rather than join the hue and cry, he hired Indians to work his ranch north of Tucson. He was engaged to an attractive young lady in Chicago named Elinor Rice, but this did not deter him from marrying Consuela Arriega. Consuela was a Mexican girl who had been brought up by Pima Indians, and the wedding ceremony was performed according to Pima custom. Walker ignored the criticism of his neighbors, and at the same time still considered himself engaged to Elinor.

He ran his ranch profitably and with a firm hand. No liquor was allowed on the grounds. Those with the smell of alcohol on their breath were banned from his house. If anyone on his payroll visited a saloon while in Tucson he was immediately discharged. The one exception to this rule was a man named Juan José Gradello, a Papago Indian who apparently surfaced in Arizona coincidentally with Walker's arrival. Gradello could get drunk, disappear for days, or just lie around in his cabin doing nothing and excite not the slightest reaction from Walker.

Often the two men would talk for hours. More often than not, the subject was silver. From the day of his arrival, Walker had heard the legend of the hidden silver mine of the Papagos and how prospectors from all over the territory had risked Indian attack for years in search of it. Walker also was searching for it, but doing it the easy way. Whether Gradello knew the location of the mine and withheld the information, or whether he was engaged in espionage among his fellow Papagos will never be known. What is known, however, is that thirteen years passed after Walker appeared in Arizona before Gradello took him to a site some miles south of the ancient ruins of Casa Grande and pointed out the source of the Papago silver.

Walker staked out a claim and named a town he planned on the site, Vekol. The name of the new community reportedly was a Papago word meaning "grandmother." The claim owners were listed as Walker, Gradello, and Colonel Peter R. Brady. Walker and Brady were listed as the founders of Vekol, and the date of the town's birth was set as February 5, 1880.

Gradello did not last as a claim holder. Approximately three months after the claim was filed, Gradello sold out to Brady and Walker for the proverbial undisclosed sum. A house was built for him in Vekol, adjacent to the more imposing structure erected by Walker, and once again Gradello became the only person exempt from the Vekol ordinances decreed by Walker. These were the same rules that applied on Walker's ranch: no liquor, not even the smell of it.

The Vekol was a profitable operation. Within a year the main shaft had been sunk to a depth of more than one hundred feet. The ore that the two partners were shipping to Kansas

City, Denver, and San Francisco was being assayed at about $2,000 a month. A year later the main shaft struck an even richer load, and Walker and Brady tripled their monthly net income. Vekol had a population of more than four hundred, and Walker, who owned the store and all of the buildings other than Gradello's home, ruled it like a fiefdom.

Walker still corresponded with members of his family and his patient fiancée in Chicago. Consuela bore him a daughter. Three years after Vekol was founded, Walker's brother Lucien appeared. John Walker did not appear particularly pleased, but thirty days after Lucien's arrival, the two brothers paid Brady $65,000 for his third interest in the mine. What convinced Brady to sell is a mystery for the *Weekly Arizona Enterprise*, which reported the transaction, disclosed also that the Vekol mine now was netting about $1,500 a day. A year later, after the construction of a stamp mill, the same newspaper reported the production of $169,807 worth of silver bullion within a three-month period. The town now had a hotel, but no saloon, a public library, a school, two churches, a livery stable, a boardinghouse, and a total population of about eight hundred.

In 1886, another brother, William Walker, arrived in Vekol. John D. Walker appeared to be more upset by William's appearance than he had been over his reunion with Lucien. William, who apparently was the youngest and most energetic of the three sons, immediately assumed a proprietary interest in the operation of both the mine and the town.

For several days John sulked and remained in his house talking only to Gradello.

"Why don't we throw them out?" Gradello asked.

John Walker shook his head. "There's more to it than that," he replied ambiguously. He rose from his chair, started to walk across the room, then suddenly staggered. He would have fallen had Gradello not caught him.

These seizures of dizziness occurred regularly throughout the afternoon and that evening, Consuela and Gradello took him by buggy to a hospital in Tucson. Here, after a few days of observation, doctors diagnosed his illness as a minor stroke. They suggested that during his recuperative period he take an extended vacation. Walker thought the suggestion a reasonable one. He decided to go to San Francisco, taking Consuela and his daughter, Juana, with him.

The day before his departure he returned to Vekol and withdrew $80,000 cash from his personal account in his own bank. Two days later, he paused in Los Angeles, long enough to deposit the money in a bank account he maintained in this Southern California city.

Lucien and William became furious over this apparent expression of distrust by their older brother. They retaliated by petitioning the federal court in Tucson to appoint them as conservators of John's estate. (Arizona was still a territory and so was under the jurisdiction of the federal government.) The court granted the petition on a temporary basis. At the same time, the court authorized the immediate incarceration of John D. Walker in an asylum where competent medical personnel could have the time and opportunity to determine the sanity of John D. Walker.

About two weeks after his arrival in San Francisco, John was picked up by United States marshals in the lobby of the Palace Hotel and was taken to the Hospital for the Insane in Napa, California. No one thought to notify his wife and daughter, who waited upstairs in a hotel suite. After her husband had been missing for two days, Consuela telegraphed his best friend for help. Shortly thereafter, Gradello arrived in San Francisco. He immediately filed a missing-person report with the San Francisco Police Department. A short time later, detectives notified Consuela and Gradello of John's whereabouts and the reason for his incarceration.

The federal court in San Francisco did not move as precipitously as the one in Tucson had. It took the lawyers Gradello hired more than a month to get John D. Walker freed under a writ of habeas corpus.

The Walker family and Gradello returned immediately to Vekol where John faced his brothers for a showdown. The outlook was bleak. During the two months that John had been gone, title to the mine and everything he owned in the town had been transferred to Lucien and William as conservators. The only property left in John's name, and thus under his control, was his home in Vekol. Lucien and William were absentee operators. During John's incarceration, they had both moved to the less confining atmosphere of Tucson.

The hostility between the Walker brothers now became public knowledge. Lucien and William petitioned the court for another order to confine John. This request was rejected by the court on the grounds that if John were so incompetent as to be unable to care for himself, he would never have been released from the hospital in Napa. On the other hand, the federal district court refused to revoke the order of conservatorship, issuing an order instead for John to show cause why the order should not be made permanent. The conflict became a battle between lawyers flailing each other with depositions.

It was after one such deposition, taken several weeks after his return, that John returned to Vekol more angry than usual. It was cold. There had been several days of below freezing weather, which made the ground hard. After dinner John went to see Gradello, but his friend was not at home.

John left a note asking Gradello to come and see him when he returned, no matter what time. It was shortly after midnight when Gradello arrived. Consuela was still up. John took Gradello into one of the bedrooms and opened a closet door. There, hidden under folded blankets, were some three hundred silver-bullion ingots, each weighing about twenty-five pounds.

"They say I am crazy because I have hoarded silver," he told Gradello. "They think I have it hidden in a vault in Tucson, and they are going to get a court order tomorrow to seize it. When they find nothing, they will search my house."

"You are crazy indeed if you keep it here, then," Gradello replied.

"Precisely," Walker said. "Now I want to borrow your wagon and your horse."

A half-hour later Gradello helped Walker load the ingots into the wagon. They worked quietly so as not to disturb the sleeping town.

"Where are you going to take them?" Gradello asked.

Walker shook his head. "If you don't know where they are you can say so truthfully if asked in court."

Gradello recalled something else that Walker said that night. "One of the grounds they are using to say I am incompetent is that I am living with a squaw. I have plans that will thwart this argument," he added, "but don't tell Consuela."

It was about two in the morning when John Walker drove off into the night with the wagon load of silver bullion. He turned north on the county road which led to Casa Grande. He had not asked Gradello to accompany him and help unload the silver, and Gradello did not volunteer such help. He waited at the house with Consuela and her small sleeping daughter, Juana.

A little after four in the morning, John Walker returned. He was in good spirits and the wagon was empty. "They are almost in plain sight," he said, "but they'll never find them."

The next afternoon, Gradello once again came over to the Walker home. John D. Walker had left. He told Consuela that the house was hers and that he would not be back. He also told her to write to him if she needed money. Gradello recalled that Consuela showed no emotion over the departure of her husband, a man to whom she had been married for more than a quarter of a century.

Walker moved to Tucson where the first steps of the court battle to win back his property were being taken. The reason that Consuela was left behind was disclosed a few weeks later when Elinor Rice arrived in the territory. After a thirty-year engagement, John D. Walker was ready to marry his fiancée. The wedding took place in Tucson on April 18, 1891. If John bothered to divorce Consuela, there is no record of it. The only record of the marriage was in the memories of a few Pima Indians who had witnessed the ceremony.

The newly married couple adjourned to a nearby health spa for their honeymoon. In no way was the honeymoon idyllic. A new federal judge had been appointed to the bench in Tucson, and the morning after the wedding John was taken into custody on another commitment order obtained by Lucien and William. Jailed in Tucson to await a competency hearing, he was rescued by his bride and his attorneys who explained to the new judge that this was the second time around on this hoked-up charge.

His freedom lasted less than twenty-four hours. This time he was arrested on a criminal complaint by Lucien and William over the embezzlement of more than three hundred silver-bullion ingots from the Vekol mine. After another night in prison, he was released on $50,000 bail. The case came to trial quickly and the charges were dismissed when the court ruled that it was a legal impossibility to embezzle one's own property.

John Walker again was summoned before Lucien's and William's lawyers for taking a deposition in reference to the pending litigation over the conservatorship. He was asked repeatedly what he had done with the silver ingots. He repeatedly refused to tell. His obstinate attitude was referred to a judge who ruled that John would be held in contempt of court unless he revealed his secret. Before the deposition could be resumed, however, John suffered another slight stroke. Lucien and William again sought a commitment order. It was granted, and this time, John was taken to Napa Hospital again for observation. On July 2, 1891, less than three months after his marriage to Elinor, John D. Walker died in the Napa Hospital for the Insane.

Thirty-one days later, Juan Gradello discovered the body of Consuela Walker lying on the floor of her home in Vekol. She had died of an apparent heart attack. Gradello took teenaged Juana home with him.

At the time of his death the estate of John D. Walker was estimated at $1.5 million, including the $80,000 in cash in a Los Angeles bank. Not included in the estimate was the three hundred silver ingots. Gradello immediately contacted lawyers to act on Juana's behalf. Apparently Elinor did not put in a claim for the estate and, according to some reports, quietly returned to Illinois. Lucien and William, however, bitterly fought Juana's claim.

The case dragged through the courts for seventeen years, with most of the estate winding up in the hands of the attorneys. In 1907 the United States Supreme court decided in favor of Lucien and William. The Supreme Court, which at that time had no interest in the rights of minorities, agreed that Juana Walker was indeed the daughter of John D. Walker and, under ordinary circumstances, should be entitled to the inheritance. What disqualified her, however, the court ruled, was the fact that she was half or one-quarter Indian. Because Arizona law decreed that marriage between Indians and whites was illegal, Juana Walker's claim was invalid.

With the death of John Walker, Vekol began to decline. The lode ran out. Its post office was shut down in 1909, and the last resident left in 1912. Today it is one of the barely discernible ghost towns that abound in Arizona.

One of the last persons to leave Vekol was Juan José Gradello. He spent years looking for the three hundred silver ingots that were hidden "almost in plain sight" somewhere near the old home of John D. Walker. The hiding place is near the old road because the ingots were taken there in a wagon. The silver had to be hidden near the house because Gradello said that John was only gone for two hours, and it would have taken him at least three-quarters of an hour to unload it.

One thousand and fifty pounds of pure silver should be worth a canvass of Vekol with a metal detector.

THE JARBIDGE INCIDENTS

There is nothing left of Jarbidge, Nevada, today. It is a ghost town located at the bottom of a canyon more than 2,000 feet deep in the northern part of the state near the Idaho border. Unlike many of its more lusty neighbors, Jarbidge never did boom.

It was founded as a gold mining camp. At its peak of prosperity, it contained only eight hundred inhabitants, six saloons, two brothels, a small hotel, and a few business shops along its main street. It served four mines of modest production and a fifth which was *almost* found in the area. The missing mine goes by the name of the Lost Sheepherder.

In the late fall of 1890, a prospector named John Ross was driven out of the Jarbidge Mountains by a snowstorm. He had been alone for weeks and hungered for human companionship. Thus, when he ran across a sheep camp run by Russ Ishman near Jarbidge, he paused to chat. Ishman was a hospitable man, and he offered Ross a shot of whiskey. This was followed by a few more, and, as Ross became more mellow, he took Ishman into his confidence.

Ross had discovered an extraordinarily rich float, he

confided, and had tracked the surface gold to a point high in the mountains before the snowfall had driven him out. (A float is made up of pieces of gold that have been washed out by natural causes from a gold vein.) Ross had left behind his pick and shovel to mark the start of the search in the spring.

Ross apparently gave some indications as to where he had left his pick and shovel because by the time the snows had melted the following spring Ishman had given up sheepherding in favor of prospecting. He found Ross's pick and shovel with little difficulty. A more disconcerting discovery, however, was that of a human skeleton with a hole in the skull lying beside the miner's tools.

Understandably, Ishman was nervous as he began his search for the source of the float. There was a strong probability that Ross was a murderer and that he would be back in the mountains very soon. Nevertheless, Ishman continued to follow the float higher into the mountains. Two weeks later, he came to its source, a lode so rich that the rock was seamed with yellow. He pried a few samples of the rock loose from the outcropping before he made camp that night.

The next morning someone shot at him. The bullet was fired from an unseen rifle, and it hit the enameled coffee cup he was lifting to his lips, ripping it from his grasp. Ishman threw himself behind a nearby boulder. His finger bled copiously where it had been cut by the handle of the coffee cup. He thought he was going to be murdered and that there was no way he could fight back. His rifle and gun were inside his small tent. If he went to get them, he would be shot down.

There was no sequel to the rifle fire, however. Hours passed. Ishman could detect no signs of any other human within sight or sound. He spent most of the day hiding behind his boulder. In late afternoon, he realized that eventually he would have to move, so he gathered the courage to dash to his tent. The move attracted no attention, but Ishman found no relief from his fear. With the arrival of dusk, he picked up his weapons and the ore samples he had taken from the rock cropping and set off down the mountain. His route took him past the skeleton, and there he paused to pick up the skull.

When he arrived in Jarbidge he told his story to John Pence, a prominent sheep rancher and one of the town's leading citizens. When the ore samples were assayed and valued at a phenomenal $4,000 a ton, Pence decided to put aside his sheepherding in favor of gold mining. Because of the obvious danger, Ishman told four other men from the town, in addition to Pence, of the discovery. A six-man partnership was formed.

In late May, Ishman guided the heavily armed party into the Jarbidge Mountains. When they reached the spot where Ross had halted his exploration the preceding fall, both the headless skeleton and the miner's tools had disappeared. The expedition paused here to allow Ishman to get his bearings.

A moment later a rifle-shot once again echoed through the mountains. This time the bullet struck Ishman in the temple killing him before his body hit the ground. His companions took cover, but the mysterious killer fired no more bullets.

The surviving members of the expedition were prudent men. Logically, they decided that Ross was the killer, and that he could be apprehended much more efficiently when he came out of the mountains. This decision was reached quickly, and Pence led the group back to Jarbidge. Word was sent to Elko about the murderer loose in the Jarbidge Mountains along with the suspicions as to his identity. A week or so later Pence received a letter from the sheriff in Elko. The killer was not John Ross. Ross had died of pneumonia apparently contracted when he passed out from drunkenness outside a saloon the preceding February.

The year following Ishman's murder, Pence and his companions once again entered the Jarbidge Mountains cautiously. They had no difficulty in reaching what they thought was the site where Ishman was murdered. They were not attacked by an unseen rifleman, but they could find no trace of the surface float that led to the fabulously rich lode found by both Ross and Ishman. As nearly as can be determined, the lode still remains to be rediscovered.

Gold was discovered in other areas around Jarbidge, however. The richest strike occurred in 1908, but it caused no great boom in the fortunes of Jarbidge. Unlike many of the earlier mining towns, Jarbidge had no boosters. The railroad ignored it. Merchants had learned through previous experience that the life expectancy of a mining town in the West was short. If the mines continued to produce, they were purchased by conglomerates that operated them with cheap, imported Chinese labor. Jarbidge was born too late to boom, and, from its inception, it adopted a funereal habit.

Because it came into existence late, Jarbidge died at a later date than many of the other mining towns. But it was not for many years after it had begun to die that anyone realized Jarbidge, in one sense, was an epitaph for the entire Wild West.

To reach the remains of Jarbidge today requires considerable driving skill. The narrow road twists and sideslips down the side of a canyon almost 2,500 feet in a distance of less than 5 miles. In 1916, when the town was eight years old, the road and the grade leading to it was even more hazardous. One reporter, who made the trip by stagecoach, described the road as less than a foot wider than the conveyance.

At least two stage drivers lost their lives on the road. One was caught in an avalanche and the other plunged off the road during a blizzard. Shipping supplies into the community was a hazardous task, especially during the winter months. According to Nell Murbarger, a prominent Western historian, residents of Jarbidge paid one hundred dollars a ton for hay, and fresh eggs were more costly than watch charms.

The road linked Jarbidge to Rogerson, Idaho, approximately sixty-five miles to the north. The stagecoach, which ran about three trips a week, usually arrived in Jarbidge about three o'clock in the afternoon. On December 5, 1916, the stage was late, but this was not considered unusual because of the weather. Shortly before noon there had been a small avalanche near the Flaxie Mine, and there had been several snow flurries during the afternoon.

Some disagreement exists over the name of the stagecoach driver. One account identifies him as F. M. Searcy. Another reports his name as Frank Slattery.

When night came, and the stage still had not arrived, the Jarbidge postmaster sent out a couple of men on horseback to look for it. They returned several hours later to report that they had ridden to the top of the pass and had seen no signs of it, nor were there any visible signs that it had skidded off the road into the canyon. The postmaster, and almost everyone else in Jarbidge, assumed that the stage either had not left Rogerson or had broken down somewhere north of the pass. The delay would affect nearly everyone in the town because the stage carried the payroll (more than $30,000) for employees of the four mines, plus $10,000 in cash designated for the town's largest gambling casino and the general store.

About noon the following day, a freight wagon from Rogerson drove into Jarbidge. The two teamsters reported that the stage had left Rogerson on schedule the preceding day. The freight wagon had followed the same route that the stage took, but had seen no sign of it. Search parties were immediately sent up the grade to look for clues to where it might have gone off the road into the canyon. A detailed search failed to turn up any indications that the stage had tumbled into the canyon, but the consensus was that this was what had happened and that the skid marks had been erased by the snow flurries and winds of the previous day.

Shortly before dusk Mrs. Dexter, an elderly widow who lived about two miles north of the center of the town, appeared in the General Store and Post Office to pick up her mail. When told that the stagecoach apparently had gone off the grade, Mrs. Dexter shook her head. "Nonsense," she replied. "It passed my house about five o'clock last night."

Mrs. Dexter was known to be a little confused at times, but she insisted that it was on the previous night that she had seen the stagecoach pass her house. "It was snowing and the driver was all slouched down into his greatcoat," she said. "If I could have caught him I would have asked him in for a cup of warm tea."

The postmaster still was skeptical, but he dispatched a couple of riders to look over the area between the town and Mrs. Dexter's outlying house. The searchers found the stagecoach in a small grove of trees about three hundred yards off the road and less than a mile from the center of town. The lead horse, nearly dead from the cold, was tethered to one of the trees. The brakes were frozen to the rim of the wheels. Frozen to the rear seat of the coach by his own blood was the driver, bullet holes in both his head and chest. The mail sacks which contained the money shipments were missing.

Investigation of the murder the following morning indicated two areas where the ambush could have taken place. One was about a mile north of the Dexter residence where tracks in the road indicated that the stagecoach had slithered from one side of the road to the other for approximately seventy-five yards. If the ambush had occurred here, it meant that the murderer had been driving the stage when it was seen by Mrs. Dexter. The other possible ambush site was at a point about fifty yards north of the small grove of trees where the stage had been hidden. Bloodstains were found there under some freshly fallen snow.

A small creek ran along the side of the grove farthest from the highway. A path had been trod into the ground by the side of the stream and a rickety footbridge had been built over it as a shortcut into town for pedestrians. Along this path and on the bridge, investigators made what they thought was a significant discovery: the footprints of both a man and a dog.

One of the miners who lived in Jarbidge was a young man named Benjamin Kuhl. He was a surly man whose only friend in the community was his dog, a large yellow mongrel. The dog was as friendly as his master was unfriendly, and it was no chore for one of the investigators to entice the animal away from his cabin and out to the grove. The paw prints in the snow matched those of the dog, according to testimony offered later.

The dog, however, pointed the finger of suspicion toward his master in a much more dramatic manner. After his pawprint had been compared, the animal bounded over to a fallen log and began barking and digging at its side. Upon raising the log, the investigators found underneath it a blood-stained shirt and coat. The shirt, a black-and-white woolen check, was similar to one often worn by Kuhl. One of the investigators also identified the coat as Kuhl's property.

The band of amateur sleuths then descended upon Kuhl's cabin. There, under the bed, they found a revolver with two shots fired from it. The records do not indicate whether or not the weapon was the same caliber as the gun used in the murder of the stagecoach driver.

When Kuhl returned to his cabin, he was arrested by his fellow townsmen and immediately taken to Elko to await trial. He denied any knowledge of the crime and claimed the gun was not his. He denied ever owning a gun. He produced witnesses at his trial who stated that Kuhl was in a Jarbidge saloon the evening of the murder. On cross-examination the witnesses were not sure which night they had seen Kuhl, even though the day-long trial was held only one week after the murder. His lawyer pointed out that Kuhl quite probably would have been stricken with pneumonia had he walked bare-chested from the spot where he allegedly buried his coat and shirt to his cabin. The jury did not accept this logic. It found Kuhl guilty of first-degree murder and, according to the custom of the day, recommended that he be hanged. The sentence was commuted by the judge, however, to one of life imprisonment. Kuhl served twenty-seven years in the Nevada State Prison in Carson City. He was released in 1944. Three days after his release, Kuhl was struck and killed by a hit-and-run driver as he was walking along the highway between Elko and Jarbidge.

The $40,000 taken in that stage robbery has never been recovered. Most of the money was in gold currency and would be worth considerably more than its face value today. If Kuhl was guilty of the robbery, then the treasure probably is hidden somewhere along the footpath (less than a mile long) that connected the town of Jarbidge to the grove of trees where the stage was hidden. It is not unlikely that Kuhl was on his way back to Jarbidge to pick up his treasure when he was killed.

If Kuhl was guilty of highway robbery and murder on the night of December 5, 1916, then history awards him a more unique distinction than that of an ordinary bandit and murderer. His act would signify the end of an era in the Wild West, for he would be the last man in its history to have held up a horse-drawn stagecoach.

THE MAN WITH HALF A NOSE

One of the most successful bandits of the Southwest was Pedro Nevarez, a cutthroat who, oddly, has attracted little attention from historians. He is better known as El Chato, which translates loosely as Pug Nose, because half of that appendage was lopped off during a cutlass fight with another desperado.

El Chato hid his band in the wilderness of the Los Organos Mountains, east of the Rio Grande in what now is southern New Mexico. For about a decade in the mid-1600s he preyed with impunity upon travelers along El Camino Real. Legend says that even the Apaches feared him. Other sources contend that half of his raiders were pure Apache and that the rest, including El Chato, were half-Apache. On several occasions Spanish troops were sent into the area to run him down, but the wily El Chato apparently received advance notice of such expeditions and retired to his mountain hideout until the danger was past.

His preferred victims were members of wagon trains

82

traveling between the garrison at El Paso and the more northern Spanish cities of Mesilla, Santa Fe, and Taos. These raids
not only provided him with jewelry and money, but also with
supplies that helped sustain his organization. He controlled a
network of spies and informers in both El Paso and Santa Fe
that, in addition to letting him know when a military expedition was being mounted against him, also told him whenever a
loosely guarded convoy with valuable cargo was headed in
either direction. El Chato also usually was aware of the route
his victims intended to take; whether it was along the old El
Camino Real or the more dangerous Jornada del Muerto, the
Journey of Death.

The latter route won its gruesome reputation from the
untold numbers of travelers who perished on it. It still was
widely used, however, because it cut out approximately fifty
miles from the journey between El Paso and Santa Fe. It
went north in a straight line from what is now Las Cruces
for a distance of approximately one hundred miles. The safer
El Camino Real followed the Rio Grande, but bulged considerably to the west of the Jornada del Muerto.

El Chato canvassed both routes. On one occasion his
band raided a northbound caravan in the morning on El
Camino Real and another southbound in the afternoon on
Jornada del Muerto. With two notable exceptions, the loot
garnered from any individual raid was not much—precious
stones taken from women, gold and personal valuables from
men—but over a ten-year span the accumulation of such booty
mounted into the hundreds of thousands of dollars. The exceptions were a shipment of gold reportedly worth a quarter-
million dollars that was being sent from Santa Fe to Mexico
City and another shipment of church valuables worth twice
as much that was being taken to Santa Fe.

The gold bullion, also the property of the Catholic Church, was lightly guarded. The wagon carrying it, part of a six-wagon convoy, headed south at Fray Cristobal along the Jornada del Muerto. A few hours later, El Chato and his band nonchalantly galloped alongside the convoy, shot two guards, and pulled out the wagon with the bullion. El Chato also tore a diamond cross from the bosom of Señora Ortega before the gang departed with the wagon.

A detachment of soldiers was sent out from El Paso. The burned hulk of the wagon was found a few miles from the ambush site, but, as usual, no trace was found of El Chato or the gold.

The second exception to El Chato's small profits was a raid on a pack train accompanied by a group of Augustinian monks. The pack train had started out from Acolmán on the outskirts of Mexico City with an ultimate destination of Taos where the monks planned to open a mission. While the train paused in El Paso, El Chato's spies learned that the pack mules not only carried the usual church supplies but also an assortment of gold crosses, baptismal urns, chandeliers, chalices, an altar cloth woven with gold thread, and a large amount of gold coin.

El Chato struck the pack train a few miles north of Las Cruces. The raid was very brief. The bandits merely galloped into the train, cut the mules loose, then herded them back into the mountains. One of the enraged and frustrated monks said later that less than five minutes elapsed between the appearance and disappearance of the bandit with only half a nose.

The Church was furious. The military sent out a detachment four days later to search for the elusive bandit, but they did not find him. This time, however, the Church officials did not accept the Army's excuses for the failure of its search mission. Without the knowledge of the El Paso garrison, the Church put together an undercover operation in distant Durango. Here a large number of soldiers were dressed as monks. A pack train was assembled and accompanied by the pseudo-monks headed north. The caravan followed the identical route and pattern of the earlier one and, while the "monks" rested in El Paso, word was leaked that the pack mules were laden with gold and silver. El Chato's spies relayed the word of the bonanza headed his way.

The bandit attacked in almost the same spot as he had in the earlier raid, but the results were much different. From under the robes of the pseudomonks came guns. Two of the soldiers were killed, and all of the bandits except El Chato were believed slaughtered. El Chato was taken prisoner. He remained in custody in El Paso for a couple of months, then was moved to Mexico City where, after a short and speedy trial, he was hanged.

Two centuries passed. Everyone had forgotten about El Chato and his raids from the Los Organos Mountains. Then, in 1877, a band of marauding Apaches attacked the mission in Doña Ana. They set fire to the church, then fled, taking with them some boxes that they apparently thought were of value. The boxes, however, contained nothing but papers, which the Indians threw to the winds on the mesa.

Among the papers that were salvaged was a copy of a letter written by a priest of the mission to the Acolmán monastery more than two hundred years earlier. The letter tells of the capture of El Chato and of the death of all but one of his followers. The survivor, according to the letter, had been left for dead, but had managed to make his way to Robledo, where he was nursed by friends. He recovered from his wounds, but on his first venture into the town was recognized by one of El Chato's victims as a bandit and was arrested. He was tried in Robledo and he asked for absolution while waiting to be hanged.

Before the rites were administered, the bandit told the priest where El Chato kept his headquarters in the Los Organos Mountains near the cave where all of the booty other than currency had been stored. There are several translations of this letter, but the differences between them are minor.

The letter describes the cave as a natural one, facing south, near the top of a hill in Soledad Canyon. A cross cut into the rock crests the cave entrance which is partially hidden by a juniper tree. To the east of the cave are three medium-sized peaks, and within sight to the north is a dripping spring. It is two hundred and fifty paces from the cave entrance to the top of the hill. From the summit, one can look down on the Jornada del Muerto for as far as the eye can see. The interior of the cave is separated into two parts connected by a short tunnel. The cave contains more coins of silver than two mules could carry, as well as jewelry, gold bullion, and the relics of Acolmán.

The letter ends with an account of three trips the priest made into the area looking in vain for the cave. He abandoned his search when he was transferred to Doña Ana.

Many copies and many translations were made of the letter, and undoubtedly there were many searches for El Chato's treasure, all of them apparently unsuccessful.

One incident concerning the treasure is told by Dr. Arthur L. Campa in his book *Treasure of the Sangre de Cristos*. It occurred about a year after the priest's letter was discovered. In the early spring of 1878, a prominent rancher near Mesilla lost some of his prize cattle to rustlers. In the area was a man known as Don Demetrio, who had been trained by

Indians as a cattle tracker and had become more efficient in this skill than his teachers. The rancher hired Demetrio to track down his missing cattle.

According to Campa, Demetrio, accompanied by two ranch hands, set off early in the morning and by noon tracked the rustlers to a deep arroyo where they discovered the cattle had been slaughtered and the beef loaded onto several pack horses. Demetrio and his men continued to follow the trail that led toward St. Augustine Pass in the Los Organos Mountains. As they climbed higher the weather turned colder, and by late afternoon it started to snow. The snowfall soon turned into a blizzard that obliterated the rustlers' trail and forced the trackers to take shelter under a rocky ledge. The men built a fire. While searching for wood to keep the fire going, Demetrio stumbled across a cave with its opening partially blocked by debris. He crawled into the opening, stood up inside, lit a tallow candle, and found to his surprise that the cave was man-made. Timber supports still remained along the walls and signs of mining pick scars were still evident in the wall. A more sensational discovery, however, was a stack of rawhide sacks piled against one wall of the cave. Demetrio cut one of the sacks open and then another only to find that they contained solid-gold bars.

The tracker said nothing about his find to his companions, nor did he mention it to his wife when he returned to Mesilla. He was canny enough to realize that a secret once told no longer is a secret. The problem he faced was how to get the gold out of the cave and dispose of it successfully. The problem was still unsolved when he went to work on a mining claim in the Sierra Blanca in the early fall. He never was able to solve it because, during the second week of his work on the claim, an explosive charge he was lighting went off prematurely, driving shards of sharp shale into his body and eyes and blinding him permanently. His loss of eyesight loosened his tongue and, upon at least one occasion, he was led back into the mountains by eastern treasure seekers in search of the cave. His handicap, however, was too great, and the cave remained lost to him.

Campa also tells of the discovery by a prospector named Ben Brown in 1916 of a cave choked with debris, but for one reason and then another, Brown did not get around to excavating the opening to see if it covered the treasure.

The last time any public notice was given to the treasure of El Chato was in the fall of 1949. The Associated Press bureau in Albuquerque, New Mexico, reported that the body of an unidentified man had been found in Los Organos, apparently the victim of a hunting accident. The body had been found near a campsite. The dead man had been shot by a high-powered rifle fired from a considerable distance, presumably by another hunter.

Duke Reed, a curious newsman and newscaster from radio station KOB in Albuquerque, called law enforcement officials in El Paso, where the body had been taken, to ask why it was unidentified.

"Because there was no wallet, no keys, or anything else of an identifiable nature on the body," he was told.

"Does this mean you possibly suspect murder?" Reed asked.

"Not necessarily," the deputy replied cautiously. "But apparently someone rolled him after he was shot." The deputy paused, then continued. "Whoever rolled him missed the best part. He had two gold bars inside an old rawhide sack in his bedroll."

Reed remembered the legend of El Chato and included

88

it in his account of the affair during his evening broadcast. This, in turn, prompted a flurry of treasure seekers to descend on the area, but if anyone found El Chato's loot, he did not announce it.

The victim never was identified. What happened to the two gold bars is also a mystery. But there are probably many more in rawhide sacks in a cave near the summit of Mt. Soledad, where the Jornada del Muerto is visible for as far as the eye can see.

MISTAKES IN MOKELUMNE

It was never very peaceful on the Barbary Coast in San Francisco. Bordellos, gambling halls, saloons, and taverns clustered around this section of the waterfront. Murders were common. Fights were frequent. It was a recruiting ground for able-bodied men who often were drugged in bars and "shanghaied" aboard a vessel as part of a crew. It also was an excellent training ground for young physicians who could pass with impunity throughout the area, because every thug on the Barbary Coast assumed that the day would come when he too would require the services of a doctor on an emergency basis.

One of these doctors was Michael Berlin. He graduated from Harvard Medical School in 1900 and came west for some excitement and adventure before settling down to a practice in Boston. He opened a small office on Lower Montgomery Street and acquired a plethora of experience in the adjacent Barbary Coast. It was early in the evening in the fall of 1902 when he once again heard the running steps followed by the pounding on his door, which always preceded an emergency call into the Barbary Coast.

This time there had been a murder in one of the saloons. The victim was a bartender named Charlie Mason who had been shot three times in the head and was quite dead by the time Dr. Berlin arrived. Mason's murderer had been stabbed twice by Mason, and was lying in a pool of blood on the floor of the saloon. He was a man in his early sixties, in excellent physical condition, and his wounds were to prove not fatal. As was the custom on the Barbary Coast, the police were not called. The witnesses to the affray had quickly disappeared. What happened to the body of the dead bartender is unknown, but the man who killed him was taken on three planks fashioned into a litter to Dr. Berlin's office where he was sewn up and bandaged.

The bartender's killer apparently thought he was much more seriously wounded than he really was, or else he was a garrulous man. He spoke English with a foreign accent and identified himself as a Russian named Slava Tyroff. He said that the dispute with the bartender arose when he saw Mason drop some knockout drops into a drink ordered by a young man. Tyroff explained that he had become furious because, some thirty years earlier, he also had been shanghaied from the Barbary Coast. According to Tyroff, he had knocked the drink from the bartender's grasp and called out a warning to the unidentified young man for whom it was intended. Mason had then picked up a knife and stabbed Tyroff, whereupon, Tyroff had pulled out a gun and shot Mason. Tyroff continued talking as Dr. Berlin worked on the wounds.

"Most men can go through their lives without killing anything more than a fish or a chicken," Tyroff said. "Now, I have killed two men."

"You don't have to tell me about it," the doctor replied.
"A doctor at the deathbed is like a priest."

"You are not going to die. You are good for another twenty years."

Tyroff was not convinced. He continued talking. He had been born in Russia and came to this country by way of Europe when he was a young man. He had arrived in San Francisco about thirty years before, long after the initial gold rush, while the Mother Lode country of California was still attracting gold prospectors. It was the lure of gold that had brought Tyroff to California, but on his arrival in San Francisco, he was penniless and knew nothing about prospecting. He got a job as a cleanup man in a gambling spot on the Barbary Coast for a dollar a day and room and board. He worked there for about two years, becoming more fluent in English, but still learning nothing about prospecting. He did save money, augmenting his salary with tips from prostitutes who worked the casino and occasionally from the gamblers themselves. Near the end of the second year he met a prospector named Harry Oversem, an older man who had come to the gambling hall with gold he had taken out of the Mother Lode country. Oversem quickly lost his newfound money at the gambling tables.

When Oversem went broke, he became friendly with Tyroff. He told Tyroff that he still knew where gold could be found in the Mother Lode country, and when he learned that Tyroff had a three-hundred-dollar grubstake, Oversem was eager to cut him in as a partner. Tyroff quit his job, and a couple of weeks later the two men struck out into the mountains from Mokelumne Hill, the infamous town where, at the height of the gold rush, men were hanged on the average of one a day. Oversem knew precisely where he was going.

He and Tyroff headed straight east from town for three miles and crossed a large mesa toward a range of sharp hills divided by three canyons. About three hundred yards from the summit of the middle canyon, they made camp next to a spring. Before the day was out, the men dug away the camouflage that covered the entrance to Harry Oversem's mine.

The mine was still productive. After the first week of work Tyroff and Oversem had unearthed about two burro loads of ore which Oversem took into Mokelumne Hill. It was Tyroff's job to stay behind and guard the mine. When he returned, Oversem gave Tyroff a twenty-dollar gold piece as his half. Tyroff was content. Twenty dollars a week was a lot more than a dollar a day, and the work was a lot healthier than what he had done in the past.

A pattern was established that continued for about six months. Oversem would leave on a Saturday, return the following day, and pay Tyroff his twenty dollars. It took six months before Tyroff attached any significance to the fact that Oversem invariably left the camp for about a half-hour every Sunday after his return. On one Sunday Tyroff suggested that he accompany his partner on his weekly stroll. Oversem decided not to take his walk.

That night Tyroff feigned sleep as Oversem stealthily left the camp. Tyroff followed him a short distance down the canyon, saw Oversem upend a heavy granite boulder, and heard the heavy clinking of coins as they were dropped into some type of metal container. They were dropped in one at a time, and Tyroff counted twenty-one coins before the shadowy Oversem struggled to replace the rock that covered his cache. Tyroff quickly returned to camp and again pretended to sleep, as his partner silently slid into bed.

As he lay awake, Tyroff's temper began to build. If each

one of the coins he had heard was a $20 gold piece, this meant that Oversem was selling the ore for about $250 a week instead of $40. If this were true, Oversem was cheating his partner at the rate of $125 a week, and there was more than $5,000 worth of gold currency in Oversem's cache. In the early morning hours, while Oversem snored softly in his bedroll, Tyroff quietly arose, picked up a sledgehammer and swung it with all his might at the skull of the sleeping Oversem. No sooner was the deed done, then Tyroff was seized by fear and contrition. The fear stemmed from the hanging he would surely face when word of the murder reached Mokelumne Hill. The contrition came from the fact that he had killed a man. The fear was responsible for his actions, however. Without waiting to pack his bedroll, he saddled the mule he and Oversem had purchased and departed. He skirted around Mokelumne Hill without even arousing a dog and by dawn was well beyond Sutter Creek. A week later he was shanghaied as an able-bodied seaman on a schooner.

He had returned to San Francisco about three weeks before the altercation with the bartender, thinking it probably would now be safe to look for the gold cache hidden by his crooked partner. But now it was too late.

Dr. Berlin helped his patient to his feet and walked him to another room where he kept a cot for such emergencies. "You can rest here for the night," he told Tyroff, "then I'll get someone to help you to your hotel tomorrow."

For the first time, Tyroff looked at him with hope.

"They are only superficial wounds," the doctor said. "One went a little deep, but it missed everything important."

Tyroff nodded and slowly lay down on the cot. "That story I just told you," he said, "I made it up. It isn't true."

For the first time, Dr. Berlin believed the tale.

Tyroff went by hack to his hotel the following morning. A week later his body was found in a Barbary Coast alley, a bullet in his head. Rumor around the Barbary Coast was that the killing had been done by a brother of the dead bartender.

The cache of $5,000 worth of gold currency intrigued Dr. Michael Berlin. In 1904 he closed down his San Francisco practice, which had been more rewarding in experience than in money, and made plans to return to Boston. Before he left, however, he decided to take a trip to Mokelumne Hill and to see if, by any wild chance, he could find Harry Oversem's cache. He took a steamer to Stockton where he rented a horse for the long trek to Mokelumne Hill.

Dr. Berlin checked into the Hotel Leger, Mokelumne Hill's only hostelry, then strolled down the street and entered a bar. The bartender was young, but there was an elderly man among the patrons. Before the doctor went searching through the mountains, he wanted to make sure that there really had been a Harry Oversem.

With some prodding the old-timer remembered. "Sure, he was one of those miners who got murdered back up yonder," he said. "I think he was the one whose body was found. Had a foreigner for a partner. Never did find his body."

"Then how do you know he was murdered?"

"Caught the fella that done it. Had Oversem's gold watch on him. A bad Mexican, he was, named Guillermo Cabrera. We hanged him right outside here. Murdered them both, he did."

Dr. Michael Berlin spent a week in the mountains east of Mokelumne Hill. He found the large mesa, the range of sharp hills divided by three canyons and the spring near the summit of the center canyon that had been described to him by Tyroff. He also found what appeared to be an old mine shaft. He did not find the cache of gold coins hidden by a cheating partner.

Mokelumne Hill looks today much as it did a century past. The Leger Hotel still stands. The main street of the town has been paved, but the stores still have their false fronts. To enter a bar is to walk into the past. It was only recently that the town council passed an ordinance prohibiting the discharge of firearms within the town limits. Somewhere outside of town there is 136 pounds of gold buried in two covered iron skillets. It belonged to an old prospector named Buster.

According to legend, the gold hoard represented Buster's life savings, accumulated at numerous washes around the Mother Lode country. Buster decided to retire on his gold in Mokelumne Hill. A few days after he built a small cabin on the outskirts of town, he decided to have his gold weighed at the general store in Mokelumne Hill. Buster was getting old and was a bit eccentric. He came into town leading his burro by a halter. Over the animal's haunches were two iron Dutch ovens and in these ovens was Buster's gold, weighing one hundred and forty pounds. Buster left four pounds on deposit at the store for credit against future purchases and returned to his cabin.

Unfortunately for Buster, the storekeeper was a talkative man. Word quickly spread around town of the peculiar containers in which the old-timer carried his gold. This information presently reached the attention of a transient badman named Smokey Hall who rushed on horseback out to Buster's cabin. Unfortunately for Smokey his interest in Buster had not been unnoticed; three vigilant citizens had followed him.

They arrived too late to save Buster, but they caught Smokey in the act of rummaging through the cabin. The body of his victim lay across the cabin threshold. Smokey was tried instantly, found guilty of murder, and was hanged from a tree in front of the cabin. The trio of vigilant citizens buried Buster in the front yard, they conducted an exhaustive search for the victim's gold in order that it might be safeguarded. There was no trace of the gold nor of the two Dutch ovens. There are no indications that it ever was found. It could not have been buried too far from Buster's cabin, for he had returned from the store with his treasure less than two hours before he was murdered.

There is still another legend of buried gold around Mokelumne Hill, and although the gold was found before it was buried, the story is worth telling as an example of the tales that circulated throughout the Mother Lode country of California.

About a century ago, the owner of the Leger Hotel left Mokelumne Hill for a month-long visit to San Francisco. He entrusted the operation of the hotel to the day clerk, a diffident young gentleman named Ely Smith, who had a penchant for gambling. One night, shortly after he had taken charge of the hostelry, Smith became heavily involved in a game of faro in one of the saloons. Three times that night, after his stake was gone, Smith returned to the hotel and replenished his bank roll with hotel funds.

He gambled nightly for several weeks, and his luck showed no sign of turning better. Eventually he reached a point where not only the hotel's cash was gone, but so was the gold stored in the hotel's safe by prospectors and semi-permanent guests. As crimes far less serious than this were hanging offenses in Mokelumne Hill, Ely Smith awoke one morning feeling very depressed as well as being very broke.

After weighing the matter most of the morning, he decided to beat the hangman to the drop. Taking a lariat from the livery stable, he walked off into the hills behind the town. Eventually he came to a large fresno tree that he climbed to fasten the rope for his suicidal hanging. After the line was fastened and the noose was made, Smith paused in the branches for some last reflections.

While he was so engaged, he heard hoofbeats and presently saw an elderly man on horseback heading in his direction. Smith drew himself back against the trunk. The stranger reined in his horse directly below Smith, looked around him, but not up, then dismounted. He proceeded to take a miner's shovel from the horse's pack and to dig a hole under the tree. Into the hole went a large leather sack. The stranger then quickly filled in the hole and carefully covered all signs of the excavation with leaves and twigs. He then rode off in the direction of Mokelumne Hill.

Smith waited for a long time after the stranger had disappeared before he climbed down from the tree. The dirt was soft and easy to loosen with his hands. Within a few moments, Smith had pulled out the sack and tumbled its contents onto the ground. The sack contained almost $3,000 worth of gold coins. Smith's depression gave way to instant euphoria, and he abandoned his planned suicide.

He raced back to the hotel, replaced the embezzled funds with the partial contents of the sack, and set the rest aside for his evening at the faro table.

Later that afternoon, he had a sudden start. The stranger who had buried the sack came into the hotel and registered as a guest. His name was Seth Powers, and he came from San Francisco. Smith quickly regained his composure. He had not been seen. There was no way Powers could ever find out who had dug up his gold.

That evening Smith's luck turned. He won back all that he had lost and more. The next day, as Powers was checking out, Smith briefly entertained the idea of returning his gold. He decided against it. It would require too complicated an explanation.

On the following day, the town marshal came into the Leger Hotel and asked if Seth Powers had been a guest there.

Smith paled. "For one night," he replied nervously. "Why?"

"Need his home address," the marshal replied. "The old man went and hanged himself from a fresno tree just outside of town. Dug a hole in the ground then hanged himself."

DIAZ'S LOST GRAVE

Not all treasures are of gold or silver, money or diamonds. Some of the most interesting are of an historical or archeological nature, such as the grave of Melchior Diaz.

The ubiquitous Jesuit priest, Father Eusebio Kino, is generally accorded the credit of being the first European to travel west of the Colorado River and the first to explore what is now Baja, California. There is, however, strong evidence that suggests that Father Kino was preceded by a detachment of Spanish soldiers led by Captain Melchior Diaz. The story starts with the Seven Cities of Cibola—the lucky seven towns purportedly built of gold—which gullible Spaniards searched for over a huge portion of North America.

One of the most ambitious expeditions in search of Cibola was launched by Vasques de Coronado, who marched overland from Mexico City to what is now Santa Fe, New Mexico. As a part of the logistics of this operation, supplies were sent north from Acapulco to the head of the Gulf of California. The small fleet carrying these supplies was com-

100

manded by one Fernando de Alarcón. The original plan called for Coronado to rendezvous with Alarcón near the mouth of the Colorado River. Coronado, however, followed the Rio Grande north from El Paso, a route that would miss the meeting point by several hundred miles.

According to the *Narratives of Casteñada*, an account of the Coronado expedition by his scribe, Pedro de Casteñada, Coronado dispatched Diaz with a forty-man team to make the rendezvous with Alarcón and bring back the needed supplies. Accompanied by impressed Indian interpreters, Diaz headed west and reached the Colorado River about one hundred miles north of the Gulf.

Here he headed south and, after a three-day journey, encountered some Indians who told him that Alarcón had sailed up the river to the present location and, after a long wait, had departed. One Indian took Diaz to a tree, dug out a clay pot from the ground beneath it, and from it drew out a letter that Alarcón had left for Coronado which said, in effect, that he was tired of waiting and was going back home.

Diaz retraced his steps, following the Colorado north to what now is Yuma, Arizona. There he forded the river and once again turned south, hoping, perhaps, to find traveling quicker on the western than on the eastern side of the river. He also hoped that he might be able to catch up with Alarcón's supply ships before they were out of sight in the Gulf.

The detachment moved south and, after a few days march, skirted an Indian village. The group had with them a small flock of sheep for food, and it was these animals, more than the soldiers, which attracted the attention of a large dog from the village.

The dog raced into the flock, scattering it in all directions. While the men went after the sheep, Captain Melchior

101

Diaz furiously raced on horseback after the dog. At one point he hurled a lance at the animal. The weapon struck the dog a glancing blow that upended the weapon at the precise instant Diaz galloped past. The pointed end of the lance ripped open Diaz's thigh from knee to groin.

Historians disagree on how long Diaz lived. Casteñada says the quick-tempered captain lived only for a few days. Baltasar de Obregon contends that Diaz lived for approximately one month. All historians agree that the injuries were fatal and that Diaz was buried where he died.

In the early 1930s Walter Henderson of Riverside, California, and some friends, set off on an exploratory trip of northern Baja. He eased his Model A Ford roadster carefully over the unpaved highway and rocky gullies that led toward San Felipe, a small fishing village about 125 kilometers south of Mexicali. A few miles south of a window-shaped rock formation known as La Ventana, he pulled the car off the road. Henderson and his companions unloaded their camping gear, filled their canteens with water from a tank in the car, and set out on foot.

Henderson had made several similar trips into this wilderness section of Mexico with no definite goal in mind other than the hope of coming across some old Spanish mine. He never found a mine. He did find countless Indian arrowheads, occasionally the powerful horns of a bighorn sheep arched over its bleached and sand-pitted skull. Sometimes he was serenaded by the screeching wail of a lynx, or he caught a fleeting glimpse of a mule deer. If a covey of quail were flushed from a sparse cluster of desert greasewood, he knew that water was close by. Occasionally he found the spring, but more often he did not.

102

On this present trip, however, Henderson had a definite objective. He had heard that there was an oasis not too far distant from La Ventana where native blue palms rose above huge granite basins of water stored from mountain runoffs after storms. On this search he failed because the map he had was crudely drawn. Later he was to learn that he had been several miles south of the oasis he sought.

The country he was in was deserted and parched. Mexican woodcutters who gather the ironwood used to fire the tortilla ovens of Mexicali and Tijuana had not yet been forced this far south. The explorers came across no signs of man after they left their vehicles, only twisted cacti writhing along the sandy ground, an occasional stubby tarote tree, or a lizard basking in the sun.

After a while the group entered an arroyo. On both sides, boulders protruded from the canyon walls like huge cancerous knobs. In some areas the distant mountains were the dark red of an ancient lava flow, while in other areas the mountains were bleached as white as the sand in the gully. By the time dusk arrived, Henderson knew he had missed the oasis he sought and picked a level spot to make camp. At night the dry clear air of Baja brought millions of stars so low to the ground that they mingled with the campfire.

The following morning the group started back on a different course to the spot where they had parked the car. They left the arroyo and hiked over a range of hills. In mid-afternoon they came across a curious pile of rocks, obviously stacked by man, set back a short distance from a steep ravine. Yet for miles in all directions there had been no other sign of humanity.

This pile of rocks was as tall as a short man, and twice as long. Its top was smoothly flat and the sides spread out toward the bottom at about a thirty-degree angle. The stones were rounded, and a cursory examination of the surrounding terrain disclosed that they had been gathered from a considerable distance.

Henderson picked up one of the rocks and turned it over. It was dark on the top; light-colored underneath. He knew a lot about rocks. The dark coating acquired by rocks in the desert is called "desert varnish." It is caused by heat from the sun, which draws the moisture out of the rocks in a capillary action. The dark deposit is left from the minerals in this water. In an arid region, such as this section of Baja where there is practically no rainfall, Henderson knew it would take hundreds of years for such a coating of desert varnish to form. The fact that all of the rocks in this cubed formation were so coated indicated that they had remained in their position undisturbed for a very long time.

Henderson knew something else about this pile of rocks: it was an ideal hibernation spot for the deadly red rattlesnakes of Baja. It was the latter part of April when these dangerous reptiles came out of hibernation. He tossed the rock back on the mound and backed away from it. For a while he studied the terrain, seeking some logical answer.

The mound had been built close to the side of the ravine through which they were descending from the hills. Unless a person came directly upon it, as they had, it would not be noticed. Thus, obviously it had not been built as a landmark. Henderson walked around it. It was then that he noticed the thick piece of ironwood leaning crookedly against one of the short sides of the pile. Lying on the ground was a smaller piece of ironwood. If the small piece ever had been lashed to the larger one, it would have formed a crude cross. Henderson and his companions decided the mound was a grave, but a remarkably elaborate one for its isolated position. Even today the Indians of Baja will immediately bury a corpse if they chance across one, but usually the burial site is marked at most by a small outline of rocks. Never had Henderson seen or heard of one built to monumental height. He studied the mysterious mound until, reluctantly, he was forced to depart to find his car before dark.

He puzzled over the origin of the mound for several years until one day, while reading Casteñada's narrative, he came across a passage that read ". . . on a height of land overlooking a narrow valley, under a pile of rocks, Melchior Diaz lies buried."

Henderson spent years searching for the grave, retracing his route from La Ventana back through this remote and desolate section of Baja, but he never was able to find the proper ravine.

It would be easier to get into the area today with a car with four-wheel drive, but permits are necessary from the Mexican authorities even to search for historical treasures.

THE WATERMAN AFFAIR

The feud between George C. Lee and Robert W. Waterman started in 1875. It was inevitable that Lee would wind up the loser because he was only a successful prospector, whereas Waterman was a crooked politician.

Lee was a big man, a caricature of a prospector. His beard was scraggly and streaked with white. He always wore dirty clothes over an unbathed body. His manners were crude and he was a loud braggart. He was suspicious of just about every person he met, an attitude that did nothing to enhance his popularity.

He came to California in the early 1850s, while still in his teens, from some city in the Northeast, obviously lured by the gold rush, which had started a few years earlier. He searched for gold in the Mother Lode country of north-central California, and it is known that he found a small vein near Volcano that he worked for about a year before he sold it.

He next turned up in Nevada where he reportedly found silver near Austin. The lode proved more profitable than the gold vein he had found in California, and Lee managed to do a considerable amount of high living in Austin before this section of the country palled. Again he sold out and this time drifted into the eastern part of Southern California. In Barstow he met an attractive Indian lass who apparently was more impressed by his size than she was repelled by his smell. They married and moved to San Bernardino, where Lee bought a house to live in when he was not prospecting. It was in San Bernardino that he met Waterman.

Waterman was the exact opposite of Lee. Dapper, well groomed, and highly articulate, it is unlikely that the two men would have nodded toward each other, had not Waterman been a politician. They met in a saloon where Lee was spending heavily and, as usual, talking loudly. The subject of Lee's discourse was a silver lode he had discovered earlier in the week. To most of the saloon patrons, Lee was a bore. He talked too loudly to be believed, and he had exhausted his subject matter.

In Waterman, however, Lee found an attentive and sympathetic listener. In the haze of good whiskey, Lee's suspicious nature was dulled. As the evening progressed, he decided that he had at long last found a true friend. Before Lee stumbled home to his patient wife, he had agreed to sell Waterman a half-interest in his newly discovered mine, and told him it was located about two miles north of present-day Barstow in the Red Mountains. The two men also agreed upon a name for their property. They would call it the Pencil Lead Mine.

The air of camaraderie between the two continued into the following week. When Waterman suggested that he be taken out to the lode before he paid the money for the half-interest, Lee agreed. A couple of days later, the two men rode out to the find. Waterman left Lee at the site and returned to San Bernardino with some ore samples. An assay disclosed that the ore tested even higher than Lee had indicated.

What happened next is something of a mystery. Some sources contend that Lee had never filed his claim—that he had gotten drunk, forgotten to do it, and after he became sober, thought that he had. Other sources say that Waterman arranged to have Lee's claim disappear from the records. In either event, the Pencil Lead Mine was registered as the sole claim of Robert W. Waterman.

When Lee returned to San Bernardino about two weeks later, he brought with him four pack mules laden with silver ore. He could find no trace of his new friend, but it is unlikely that he conducted much of a search for him. The ore was assayed at almost twice the value of the first samples he had brought back, and he gloated in one saloon that it was lucky he had not signed an agreement to sell a half-interest in his mine to Waterman. The mine was twice as valuable as he had first thought, Lee bragged, and so, friend or no friend, Waterman would just have to come up with twice as much cash for his half-interest.

Two weeks later, Lee departed once again for his mine. He was prepared for a long stay, for this time he brought with him twelve pack mules and provisions sufficient to last six weeks. His stay, however, was exceedingly brief. As he pulled up to his claim he was met by three men carrying rifles. One of them pointed with the muzzle of his gun toward a sign which warned against trespassing.

"It's my claim," Lee said carefully. "I've got it registered all proper."

"Not this one, you don't," one of the armed men replied. "You'd better go back and look."

"If it ain't mine, then whose is it?"

"Bob Waterman's," the gunman said.

Lee, understandably, was furious, but there was nothing he could do with three armed men facing him. He found out a short time later that there was nothing he could do in San Bernardino either. The claim was legally registered in Waterman's name. Waterman could not be found. Lee went to the sheriff to report the claim jumping. The law enforcement official was sympathetic, but pointed out that the claim legally was Waterman's. He said also that Waterman had complained to him about the theft of silver ore from the Pencil Lead Mine and identified Lee as the principal suspect.

The prospector next went to an attorney who told him also that he had no recourse legally. He recommended that Lee abandon his announced plans of hiring some gunslingers to retake the claim by force.

The irascible prospector told his story loudly and often around the San Bernardino taverns, but because of his manner and his general unpopularity, he found few sympathizers. Word of Lee's constant complaint, however, did come to Waterman's attention, irritating him to the point where he reacted by filing a suit for slander against Lee.

Instead of shutting up, Lee was delighted. "When we get to court, I'll prove he is a crook," he boasted happily.

A few weeks later, Waterman dropped the suit. The feud, however, continued. Lee made his accusations against Waterman repeatedly and monotonously to anyone who would listen. Apparently the only person who paid any attention to him was Waterman, who was becoming increasingly angry. "Lee will have to be taught a lesson," he told a friend. "I have just about reached the end of my patience."

Lee, meanwhile, had just about reached the end of his

bankroll. He resumed his prospecting, but was never gone for more than a couple of weeks. When he was in San Bernardino he did not let up in his harangue against Waterman.

About a year after his claim at the Pencil Lead Mine had been jumped, Lee found another lode. The ore that he brought back to the assayer had an even higher silver content than that of his previous discovery. Word of his strike spread quickly around the city. "I ain't goin' to register it here," Lee announced in one of the taverns. "Bob Waterman's just waiting to steal another one like he stole the Pencil Lead Mine."

A short time later, Lee rode into Los Angeles where the only man whom Lee considered trustworthy lived. Lee's friend was a crippled assayer named Sam Stewart, a man confined to a wheelchair as the result of a gun duel a few years earlier. Ever since the accident Stewart had kept a finely detailed diary of each day's activities.

"George Lee came into the office after the noon meal," Stewart wrote. "He has made a very good strike near Old Woman Springs and he wanted to register his claim here. He doesn't have any faith in San Berdoo [sic] officials because they erased his claim on the Pencil Lead. I told him that he would have to register his new claim in San Berdoo because that is where Old Woman Springs is. I told him to bring along a witness and demand a certified copy of the filing, but he thinks he can still be swindled. He smelt bad."

Lee decided not to register his new claim, preferring to protect his find by keeping its location secret. The prospector could not refrain from boasting about his strike, however.

For the next several months he would bring in his mules laden with silver ore, then in the bars he would boast that his new strike was so rich that soon he would have silver doorknobs and silver stairs in his home. He also stated loudly

110

to all within hearing distance that his mine's location was a secret because otherwise it would be stolen by Bob Waterman. On one occasion, when told he was wrong about Waterman, Lee replied that at least twice he had been followed as far as Old Woman Springs by Hans Hoffman, one of the gunman who had driven Lee away from the Pencil Lead Mine. This charge was remembered by many in the ensuing weeks.

On a Monday morning, Lee once again left San Bernardino en route to his secret mine. The following morning, two horsemen, whose names have been lost in history, approached Old Woman Springs. Before they entered the grove of eucalyptus and willows that surrounded the spring, a horse and rider raced out of the grove and headed north toward Barstow.

Near the spring, the travelers found a man lying on the ground, a large bloodstained rock in his hand. At first, they thought the man was dead, but when they dismounted they could see no signs of injury other than blood on his shirt. He was breathing, and as one of the travelers bent over him, he smelled fumes of whiskey, and realized the man was dead drunk. A few minutes later, they discovered another body. It had been dragged under a willow tree. This man was quite dead. The back of his skull had been battered to a pulp. The two travelers proceeded to tie up the unconscious drunk, then one galloped to San Bernardino to notify the sheriff while the other remained behind to guard the murder suspect.

It was a long day for the unidentified traveler. About noon the drunk sobered up enough to ask for another drink and then fell asleep again before the request could be granted. The traveler looked around for horses on which the murderer and his victim could have arrived. At the eastern end of the large grove he found three hobbled mules under some cottonwood trees.

111

Shortly before dusk Sheriff John Buckhart and three deputies arrived at Old Woman Springs. The suspect was awake and begging for a drink.

"What's your name?" Buckhart asked.

"Hoffman. Hans Hoffman."

The sheriff pointed with his thumb toward the body. "Why did you kill him?"

Hoffman shook his head and swallowed rapidly.

"You want a drink?"

Hoffman nodded and a tear rolled out of an eye. "It's a mistake," he said. "Waterman just wanted him beat up until he told us where his lode was."

"Who is he?"

"George Lee."

Hoffman's horse had run away, so Hoffman was tied on one of Lee's mules and Lee's body was slung over another mule.

As the sheriff and his deputies were preparing to leave, they heard the sound of galloping horses approaching the springs. It was dark and cloudy and the new arrivals were well into the grove before they were aware that anyone was there. Then someone cried out. The group turned their mounts, ignoring Buckhart's shout to halt. One shot was fired. One of the newcomers screamed and fell from his saddle. Still holding his gun, the sheriff walked over to his victim. He had been shot in the leg. Buckhart struck a match. He did not have to ask who this man was. He was Regis Brown, a sometimes bodyguard for Robert Waterman and foreman of his ranch in Barstow.

Hoffman was charged with murder. Some of the best legal talent in the state appeared in San Bernardino as Hoffman's defense attorneys, and it was acknowledged that the fees were being paid by Waterman. Hoffman changed his story. His defense was that Lee attacked him when they happened to run into each other at Old Woman Springs. The sheriff testified about the admission Hoffman had made while he was first interrogated at the grove. The first trial set a record for longevity in San Bernardino, lasting for more than six months. It finally was declared a mistrial when the jury hung eleven to one for conviction. A second trial followed. This was of a much shorter duration, but the results were the same as the first one; a hung jury voting eleven to one for conviction.

After this, Hoffman was released under $15,000 bail while awaiting his third trial. Two days after he was released, he vanished permanently.

Lee's wife then sued Waterman for damages resulting from her husband's death and won a judgment for $300,000, an incredibly large sum a century ago. As soon as this case was concluded, Waterman was sued again, this time by his own brother. This suit contended that Waterman had cheated the brother out of his third-interest in the Pencil Lead Mine. The brother died before the case was brought to trial, but the suit was continued successfully by his heirs who were awarded a third of the mine's profits by a sympathetic jury.

Waterman continued on with a successful political career despite his adversities in the San Bernardino courts. In 1886 he ran for lieutenant governor of California and was elected. The following year he became governor when the incumbent, Washington Bartlett, died.

George Lee's lost silver lode near Old Woman Springs has never been found. Searchers quite possibly have been confused over a switch in names. Several years ago someone decided that the name Old Woman Springs was too parochial for such a beautiful spot and the name was changed to Cotton-wood Springs. Another few years passed. A rancher decided it was a pity that the colorful names of the Old West were disappearing. He named some springs on his property Old Woman Springs.

The Old Woman Springs on a present-day map are not the Old Woman Springs where the irascible George Lee was slain a hundred years ago. He died in Cottonwood Springs, and it is near there that the rich silver lode might be found.

LOST GOLD IN UTAH

When Brigham Young led his flock of persecuted Mormons from Nauvoo, Illinois, to the West, and came to the shores of the Great Salt Lake, historians assert that he exclaimed: "This is the place." The temporary site of the Mormon Church became the site of present-day Salt Lake City.

It is unlikely that the Mormon pioneer knew at the time that Spanish explorers had said a similar thing a couple of centuries earlier when they arrived in the area and found one of the more productive gold mines in the North American hemisphere. When Brigham Young did find the gold mine, however, he quickly spread the word among the faithful to warn prospectors in the area to keep away.

"We cannot eat silver and gold. Neither do we want to bring into our peaceful settlements a rough frontier population to violate the morals of our youth, overwhelm us by numbers, and drive us again from our hard-earned homes," he announced.

The fabulous missing mine has had a variety of names: the Indian, the Ute, the Walker, the Spanish, the Mormon, the Rhodes, and the Brigham Young. The last name is the most common, probably because he was the last man to work the mine.

The Spanish were the first, and once the gold was discovered, they worked the mines in the customary Spanish manner. Soldiers rounded up hundreds of Ute Indians and forced them to work in the mine as slaves. Unlike some Indian tribes farther to the south, the Utes were not docile, and they did not succumb to the blandishments or threats from the priests brought in to rule them. A state of continual warfare existed between the Utes and the Spaniards for almost two decades in the mid-seventeenth century, when the mine was first operative. For every Spanish soldier killed, however, a dozen Utes died, primarily from overwork and malnutrition.

The ore was packed out only twice a year because of the severe winter weather at high altitudes and the extreme heat at the lower levels. During the late spring and early fall an extraordinarily large mule train, heavily guarded by Spanish soldiers, would take the long trek to Sonora where the ore was smelted.

In the spring of 1680, about two days after the ore train had set out on its semiannual southern journey, it was attacked by a large band of Utes, and every soldier and Spaniard in the convoy was slain. The ore was spilled along the trail and approximately one hundred mules were herded into Ute corrals. A couple of days later the same band of Utes successfully raided the mining camp, killing all the Spaniards. Their bodies were thrown into the mine shafts and the openings were blocked with debris. There remained only a mopping-up operation. In the early fall the northbound mule train was ambushed about a day's journey from the mine, and the Utes left no survivors. Legend tells that the Spanish twice tried to reopen the mine, but on both occasions met the same fate as the other Spaniards. The Utes had no use for the gold, but from one generation to the next they told each other of the location of the mine and of the white man's greed for the precious metal.

The Mormons' attitude toward the Indians was much different from that of the Spanish. They called the Indians "Lamanites," believing them all to have had common ancesters originating in Jerusalem in 600 B.C., and the Book of Mormon teaches that American Indians are descended from the lost tribes of Israel. The Utes did not subscribe particularly to this concept of their origin, but they approved of the Mormons' belief in it because it resulted in the most harmonious relation they ever had experienced with white men. Instead of being attacked, they were fed. Rather than being forced into slave labor, they were paid in goods such as clothing and livestock. The Mormons were not prospectors. Their collective efforts were directed toward colonizing, cultivating, and proselytizing. But eventually Brigham Young discovered that he needed gold.

Within a few years of the founding of Salt Lake City, the migration to the West prompted by the California Gold Rush was gathering momentum. Many of the wagon trains came through the Mormon State of Deseret and stopped to rest in Salt Lake City.

The wagon trains often carried manufactured goods and supplies needed by the Mormon community. Some pioneers would trade for foodstuffs. Others, of a more commercial mind, would insist upon gold or cash in payment. On one occasion, a Ute Indian overheard a traveler demanding only gold in payment for some shovels. A short time later, a Ute chief named Walkero visited Brigham Young. He carried with him several "chunks" of the almost pure gold. Because of the Mormons' demonstrated friendship with the Utes, Walkero said that he would disclose to Young the location of a gold mine in the nearby mountains. This mine had been operated by other white men many years ago, but they had been driven away by the Utes.

There was a conditional clause to Walkero's offer. Brigham Young would have to arrange for the mining to be done only by Mormons, and the mine's location would be kept a secret from all but those actually engaged in the mining operation. The Mormons could be trusted, the Ute chieftain said, but other white men could not. The miners would be under the constant surveillance and protection of the Utes while they worked. In return for this the Mormons would agree to continue feeding any Ute Indian who was in need and came to Salt Lake City for help. Brigham Young thought the agreement a good one, and both he and Walkero sealed the oral contract with one hand upon the Book of Mormon.

Young was not greedy for gold. He wanted only enough to trade for supplies and he decided that it would require only the efforts of two men to gather this amount. Consequently, he summoned a man named Thomas Rhodes and his son, Caleb Baldwin Rhodes, to his home. Here he swore them to secrecy, told them of the mine, then sent them off with Indian guides. When they returned several days later, their pack mule carried ore so pure that it almost could be used in its natural state. Caleb described it as "gold bearing rock rather than rock bearing gold." He mentioned also that the ore was taken from an existing mine.

Brigham Young wanted no gold rush to his State of Deseret, an occurrence that surely would have come to pass had he used gold ore and nuggets to purchase his supplies. He, therefore, built a small smelter and stamping press with which he issued gold currency from Deseret. Apparently, no one ever questioned him about the origin of the gold.

For approximately three years the arrangement with

the Utes worked smoothly. Then, two Utes stole a couple of horses from the Mormon settlement of Nephi. The Mormons took the incident much more seriously than did the Indians, and after catching one of the thieves, they tied him to a post and flogged him. The Utes took this as a collective insult and, in retaliation, they raided the communities of Springville, Pleasant Creek, Monti, and Nephi, stealing a large number of horses and cattle. The Mormon militia raced after the Utes, caught up with one band, and in the ensuing fight both sides suffered casualties.

Eventually Brigham Young and Chief Walkero met in Salt Lake City and made peace, but the relationship between the Mormons and the Utes was never again the same. Walkero rescinded his agreement to allow the Mormons access to the mine.

Some sources say that Caleb Rhodes occasionally slipped into the area and picked up a few nuggets, but he kept the secret of its location until shortly before his death. When he realized he was dying, he drew a crude map on a piece of buckskin. The map is so vague, it is almost worthless. A small lake is shown in the lower right-hand corner. Two lines labeled "trails" veer upward toward the right, then one makes a sharp angle to the left ending at a spot marked "gold." Three crosses in the center of the map are believed to designate a mountain range. On the left side of the buckskin is a curving line which is identified as "Rock Creek."

This map is still in existence, and there is strong evidence that it was drawn by Caleb Baldwin Rhodes. It was last known to be in the possession of a Utah mining prospector named Benjamin H. Bullock. A copy of the map appeared in the *Uintah Basin Standard* in its issue of July 10, 1958, along with a story of the mine and the following affidavits:

119

TO WHOM IT MAY CONCERN:

To the best of my knowledge, the following is a true history of the Rhodes Mine Map, a copy of which I have in my possession.

The original map from which I made this copy on paper was made on a small piece of buckskin about as large as one's hand and was owned by Ortiza Rhodes who was slain by Indians and robbed of his map. The Indians then brought it to Price, Utah, and traded it back to the Rhodes family.

Living with the Rhodes family at that time was a young man named Jake Colbert who got it from a member of the family. My husband, Warren Sulser, quite some time later, secured it from Mr. Colbert and I became its owner when Mr. Sulser passed away.

> (ss) Mrs. Mary Sulser Steele
> I am in my 85th year
> Witnesses:
> (ss) Ray D. Steele
> Ben H. Bullock

TO WHOM IT MAY CONCERN:

My stepfather, Frank Horsley, told me that he had personally seen Caleb Rhodes come into Price from his mine in the Uintah Mountains with a pack donkey loaded with a bag of rich gold ore on each side; and that he had personally taken some of the ore from the bags and examined it with his hands.

> Signed and witnessed at Goshen,
> Utah, this 18th day of June, 1958
> Mrs. Mary Sulser Steele
> I am in my 85th year
> Witness:
> Ray D. Steele

120

If Bullock ever found the lost mine, he has kept its discovery a secret. Shortly before Bullock collected his affidavits, however, there is a possibility that a Salt Lake City hunter named Clark M. Rhoades may have stumbled on it accidentally. His discovery was kept secret for more than a decade until it was revealed by his son, Gale, writing in the July/August 1967 edition of *Desert* magazine.

In the late fall of 1956, Rhoades was deer hunting in an area east of Heber City in the Uintahs. When he came across some fresh bobcat tracks in the snow, he followed them to the animal's den. The wildcat's lair was one of two very old mine shafts. At this time, Rhoades did not enter either shaft because the snow inside was deep; he had no flashlight and no desire to tangle with bobcats in the dark.

During the following summer, however, he returned to the area. The bobcats were gone, so he was able to study the mine shafts more carefully. He decided they had been deliberately filled-in years earlier or had collapsed during the passage of time. Outside the shaft he found three or four old Spanish shoulder yokes that had been used to haul ore up from the shafts. He also gathered up several ore samples from the ground which, when assayed, disclosed a heavy gold and silver content. He made no attempt to dig in the shafts for fear the blockage covered a much larger shaft into which he could easily fall.

Gale Rhoades visited the area again in 1964. He describes it as being located only a mile and a half up a mountain. He discovered that the shafts were connected about twenty feet from the entrances and, like many other Spanish mines, the shafts had been constructed in such a manner that steps had been formed near the top. The blockage in one shaft was about ninety feet down, and about an additional thirty feet in the other shaft. Cautiously, he started to dig in the deepest shaft. About three feet down he uncovered a hoisting brace, grooved from the burn of ropes. He also discovered that the dirt was becoming softer, indicating that the mine had been deliberately plugged, and posing the threat of collapse. Rather than risk a possible fall of hundreds of feet, Rhoades reluctantly abandoned his excavations.

If someone finds the time and a way to safely dig through the plugs, it should be easy to determine whether or not this is the lost Brigham Young—Rhodes, Walker, Spanish, Mormon, Ute—mine. If there are a large number of skeletons in the bottom of the shafts, then it is the lost mine where the Spaniards were buried.

There is an interesting companion story to this legend of the lost Spanish mine in Utah. The United States Army spent more than three years looking for it, not because it wanted the money, but because it wanted to destroy the Mormon hierarchy. In 1862 an egotistical U.S. Army general named Patrick E. Conner arrived in Utah with a detachment of California volunteers, and established Fort Douglas, east of Salt Lake City. Conner was unable to find any signs of plural marriage. This, plus the lack of proper deference shown him by Mormon leaders, quickly engendered a hatred on his part for all Mormons.

He knew that Brigham Young had knowledge of and access to an abundant gold mine, but no matter how much he threatened and blustered, he could not get a clue from the wily religious leader as to its location. The general then tried to break the Mormon control of the territory by spreading word that the area was indeed rich in silver and gold. He detailed his troops to prospecting duty and organized mining districts in the Jordan and Tooele valleys. He hoped to trigger a gold rush that would fill the area with prostitutes, miners, and gamblers, thus forcing the Mormons into a minority status. He circulated tracts, at government expense, pointing to the evidence of mineral resources in the territory and the great opportunities for those "opening up the country to a new, hardy, industrious population." There were few takers because none of his soldiers found any gold or silver or the fabulous lost Spanish Mine.

The failure of his first tract prompted the circularization of a more inflammatory one, again printed and distributed with the use of military funds.

> My policy is to invite hither a large Gentile population sufficient by peaceful means and through the ballot box to overwhelm the Mormons by force of numbers and thus wrest from the church, disloyal and traitorous to the core, the absolute control of temporal and civic affairs. With this in view, I have bent every energy, both personal and official, toward the discovery and development of the mining resources of the Territory using without stint the resources of every soldier of my command.

Conner also posted a reward of $5,000 for information resulting in the discovery of the lost Spanish Mine. There are unconfirmed reports that on two occasions, a Ute Indian actually collected the reward, then slipped away from Conner and his troops while "leading" them to the location.

The general finally was recalled to Washington and promoted to some obscure post. The transcontinental railroad, when it was joined at Promontory Point north of Salt Lake City in 1869, did open up Utah's ranges to mining. Gold, silver, copper, lead, and later uranium were found in the mountains, but the old Spanish Mine still is missing.

MASSACRE IN SAN MIGUEL

The Mission of San Miguel, the Archangel, located about nine miles above Paso Robles on the central California coast, is the site of one of the most grisly mass murders in the state's history. The murderers were looking for gold. They did not find it at the mission, and neither has anyone else.

San Miguel Mission was founded by Father Fermin Lasuen on July 25, 1797, the sixteenth in the series of missions built a day's journey apart in California. The small mud-roofed church, which was replaced by a larger building the following summer filled in the gap between the missions at San Antonio and San Luis Obispo. In the ensuing nine years the mission grew into a complex of several buildings including granaries and workshops, which were the center of a village of more than one thousand inhabitants.

In 1806 a disastrous fire raged through the mission, razing all of the buildings except for a part of the original church. More than six thousand bushels of grain and almost a

125

decade's accumulation of hides, wool, and cloth were destroyed. Help was sent to San Miguel from other missions, and within a year the mission, except for the church, was again operating normally. When the time came to rebuild the mission, the padres wanted a structure that would be permanent, one with a tiled roof and thick, fireproof adobe walls. It took eight years to gather the tile and make the adobe bricks and another two years to build the church. It was during this period that New Spain broke away from Spain and proclaimed itself the Republic of Mexico.

Independence had a far-reaching effect upon all of the California missions. Funds and supplies for the missions no longer came from Mexico City. The missions not only had to support themselves, but also the colonists and soldiers within their territories. Eventually, the Mexican government initiated long-delayed orders to secularize the missions.

The theory behind secularization was that the missions had completed their assignment to civilize the Indians and now could be replaced by a more politically manageable system of pueblos.

San Miguel was the last of the California missions to be secularized. The order for confiscation was signed by Governor Pio Pico in the capital at Monterey in August 1834. For the next decade, San Miguel was operated by a succession of bureaucrats. The livestock disappeared. The Indians drifted away. Eventually there was no one to grow the corn for the granaries. The mission was abandoned, except for a couple of priests. Three days before California was surrendered to the United States in 1846 at Monterey, Governor Pico sold the entire mission, except for the priests' quarters and the church, to an English adventurer named William Reed. The total price for the property was 300 pesos, or less than $250.

Bill Reed was a tall and handsome man who had arrived in California as a seaman some two years earlier and had jumped ship in Monterey. There he married Maria Antonia Vallejo. When his wife's uncle, Petronillo Rios, suggested to Reed that they go into partnership, buy the mission, and use it as a headquarters for a hacienda and also as a commercial center, Reed thought the idea an excellent one. The ranching part of the operation complemented the general store. Indians returned to work, and Reed and Rios prospered, then grew rich as gold miners swept into California.

The former mission was approximately halfway between Los Angeles and San Francisco, and it was a perfect stopping place for travelers journeying between the two cities. Reed sold them lodging, board, and provisions and would take only gold in payment. He called the money that the miners paid him his very own "lode." The usual reticence attached to the English was not a part of the cocky Reed's character. He overstated rather than understated. On one occasion he announced that he had paid 300,000 pesos for the mission and that he had recouped his investment within the first year. Understandably, Reed was a strong Anglophile, and on those occasions when an Englishman would chance through San Miguel, he usually was given the hospitality of the house on a complimentary basis.

There were no banks in San Miguel and Reed often commented that he did not need one; that he had found a hiding place for his mounting hoard of gold that defied detection. The size of his "lode" varied in his stories and, because of this, there were many who discounted the existence of any hoard at all. There were others who knew better. They knew the prices Reed charged could not bring anything other than huge profits. These were the people who noticed the bulging

127

chamois bag of twenty-dollar gold pieces that Reed carried with him. Often, near the end of a week, when the bag became too full to hold another coin, Reed would leave the mission and return ten minutes later. The bag would be empty save for a few small coins needed for change. Reed would make no secret of where he had been. "Had to go out to my safe and add a little more to the lode," he said more than once. "I'm different from most of the miners. I put my gold back into the ground instead of taking it out."

On occasion, he would be followed when he left the saloon, but always sensing when this was happening he would turn back.

For five years Reed and Rios prospered. By that time Reed had a four-year-old son named Petronillo, a daughter named Concepción, and another baby on the way. Reed and his family lived with six servants in a large building adjacent to the mission, a former warehouse that he had remodeled into a comparatively luxurious home.

One cool winter afternoon five men rode into San Miguel from the north. They were not used to horses, and if the animals had been anything other than broken-down nags, the strangers would obviously have been unable to remain mounted. Reed watched them bounce up to the mission. His first impulse was to refuse them entrance. He quickly changed his mind, however, when one spoke to him. His accent was British, a lower-class cockney but, nevertheless, British. The other strangers spoke with the same accent as they slid down from their horses. Reed immediately welcomed his fellow countrymen and escorted them inside.

He fed them and gave them drinks, and as the liquor mellowed the strangers' tongues, Reed discovered that they were all British seamen who had deserted their ship in Mon-

128

terey. They had "found" the horses all saddled outside a saloon and did not appear concerned when Reed told them that this might be considered a hanging offense if they were caught. One of the sailors, however, as a precaution, went outside and turned the animals loose, but the tired horses remained at the hitching post.

As the evening wore on, Reed confided to his newly found friends that he also had jumped ship in Monterey. He told them also of the fortune he had made in only five years. He showed them his chamois bag, heavy with gold, and repeated his tired joke of putting the gold back into the ground rather than taking it out.

"Where?" asked one of the sailors.

Reed smiled and shook his head. Another of the sailors stood up and walked behind Reed. The tavern was now deserted but for the English.

"Where?" asked the sailor again.

"That's a family secret," replied Reed, still apparently unaware of his danger. His choice of words was tragic.

"Then we'll ask your family," the sailor replied. The man standing in back of Reed pulled a dirk from its scabbard and plunged it into Reed's neck killing him instantly.

Reed's murder was the start of an insane, drunken slaughter. The quintet raced to Reed's bedroom where they woke the pregnant Maria. They demanded to know the hiding place of the gold, and when Maria screamed that she did not know, she was stripped, raped, and then stabbed to death.

The other victims of the gang murderers were killed because they might identify the killers. They included everyone staying in the mission and the Reed house. The next two to die were Concepción and the young Petronillo, followed in rapid succession by a midwife, her married daughter and grandchild, a servant and her son, a sheepherder, his wife and child, and another servant. The death toll was thirteen.

In a smaller house, a few hundred yards from the mission and the Reed house, lived Ramón Rodriguez with his wife and two sons, aged eight and four. When the screams of the killings awakened him, he immediately sent his family to hide in a growth of tall mustard weed that covered several acres nearby. He then crept up to the mission, keeping out of sight in the shadows. He saw one of the sailors carrying the nude body of Maria into the tavern. Rodriguez then took off at a dead run for the ranch of James M. Price, some three miles away. One of the sailors heard his running steps and started in pursuit, but could not match the fleet Rodriguez.

The sailor returned to the tavern, gathered together his companions, and within a few minutes they were on the trail headed south. Rodriguez heard them as they passed him in the dark.

Price and a friend, F.Z. Branch, returned to the mission with Rodriguez about an hour later. Twelve of the bodies were lying on the floor of the tavern. The body of the sheep-herder had been dropped just outside the door. Oil-soaked straw and rags had been set afire inside the tavern, but had burned out too quickly to set fire to the structure.

The three men rounded up a posse and took off in the morning. Rodriguez accompanied the posse despite the fact that his four-year-old son had become lost during the night. The search for the killers went on for days. The posse was made up of experienced horsemen who either did not know or did not take into account the fact that the men they sought could only cover a few miles before being forced to rest.

The posse had almost reached Santa Barbara when they decided that the murderers had escaped. On their way back to San Miguel, however, they ran headlong into the killers near what is now Guadalupe. Somehow the posse had passed its quarry during the chase.

During their flight the sailors had picked up sidearms, but they were slow in drawing them. They apparently had not anticipated a posse coming from the south. The gunfight was brief. When it was over, three men were dead. One sailor was fatally shot, another drowned when his horse bolted into the sea. The third victim was a member of the posse, Ramón Rodriguez. The body of his four-year-old son was found a few months later in the mustard weed near the mission, raising the total death toll to seventeen, including the two sailors.

The three surviving sailors did not live long. They were taken to Santa Barbara where they confessed, were tried, and hanged.

After the Reed massacre, San Miguel Mission slowly deteriorated. Finally, on the verge of collapse, the mission was returned to the church by court order in 1859, but it was not for another nineteen years, in 1878, that the church was reactivated. Some of the buildings were restored at this time, and a few more were rebuilt in 1901. The Franciscans assumed control in 1928 and used it for a parish church and monastery. Today it is open to the public.

The bodies of eleven of the victims of the Reed massacre are buried in one grave near the rear door of the mission sacristy. What happened to the other two bodies is a mystery. Also a mystery is the location of Reed's "lode," where he put his gold back into the earth.

THE LOST EVANGELISTS

There are many tales of lost missions, and in many cases there are records to substantiate them. One of them, possibly the Santa Isabel, was found, photographed, and then lost again. Another, the San Dionysius, appears on several old maps, but although its location is known exactly, no trace of it exists today.

One of the more intriguing of the lost-mission legends involves the Mission of the Four Evangelists. If there is written record of this mission, it has been lost in the files of the diocese in Guadalajara. Perhaps the mission was officially given a name other than the one it is called today by the Papago Indians. What makes the Mission of the Four Evangelists so intriguing is that periodically over the centuries it reappears briefly and that less than half a day's journey from it lies a fortune of gold buried beneath the skeletons of two Papago Indians.

The Mission of the Four Evangelists probably was located on the shores of the Laguna Prieta somewhere between Tinajas Altas on the Arizona-Mexican border and the tiny town of El Doctor on the southern fringe of the Gran

Desierto in Mexico. A railroad line cuts through this vast North American Sahara from Caborca on the southeast to Mexicali on the northwest. The only other thoroughfare through this devastating wasteland is the old Camino del Diablo that stretches from Sonoyta to San Luis, a small border town a short distance south of Yuma, Arizona.

Two small bodies of water interrupt the endless miles of desert sand. One is a series of three pools, known colloquially as tanks, located in a jumble of large boulders high above the highway on the northern flank of the desert. This place is named Tinajas Altas. Its cavities, eroded in granite strata one above the other, catch the runoff from rare rains and a spring that functions sporadically. The other body of water is the Laguna Prieta, a brackish lake surrounded by fresh water seeps lying in the middle of naked sand dunes. Various maps show different locations for Laguna Prieta, but most cartographers place it about fifteen miles east and eight miles south of San Luis. Explorers have gone here, however, and found not a trace of Laguna Prieta or the lost mission.

One explanation for its elusiveness is the phenomenon of the "walking hills" that surround it. Rising as high as three hundred feet above the desert floor, the sand dunes change their shape and size with each passing gust of wind. Within each of these hills there is a "heart." It may be a root or a rock, or a lost mission, but there is always a barrier to collect the windblown grains of sand. These particles of sand accumulate in hills that grow larger and larger. Then a fierce desert windstorm will lift the sand from one side of the dune and sweep it over the top to the other. When the storm subsides, the dune has taken on another shape. Often the "heart" of the dune is exposed briefly. This is why the Mission of the Four Evangelists and Laguna Prieta suddenly reappear. They

133

disappear again as the winds slowly cover them up with sand.

The most recent sighting was made from the air in 1970 by a student pilot, Masa Nakagawa, of Los Angeles, while on a cross-country solo flight. He became lost, veered to the south, and inadvertently flew into Mexico. He descended to a low altitude to get his bearings and soon, after deciding that he was too far to the south, noticed a belfry tower jutting out of the sand. He circled it a couple of times before heading north. When he landed at Tucson later, he reported the sighting, but no one had heard of a lost church.

"It was one of the times I have regretted being one of those rare Japanese who is not permanently attached to a camera," Nakagawa said.

The only known sighting of the Mission preceding Nakagawa's experience occurred in 1915 when it was rediscovered by a band of Papago Indians. The story was told by the late Juan Orosco of Quitobaquito who, at the time, was a youth of fifteen living with his family on the banks of the Colorado River. Late one afternoon a white man stumbled into the Papago village. He said he had been prospecting in an area about thirty miles away and, after deciding to move on, had packed his gear on his mule. The mule had bolted and disappeared. The Orosco family took the prospector into their home, fed him, and let him rest for a couple of days.

When they awoke on the third morning their guest was gone. A short time later the Oroscos discovered that one of their best horses, a saddle, and a rifle were also missing. In something of a switch on the usual chase in the Old West, a posse of Indians was rounded up, including fifteen-year-old Juan, and the band set off in pursuit of the felonious prospector.

In the early stage of the pursuit they followed his tracks easily. He had headed in a straight line into El Gran

Desierto. In the forenoon, however, the wind came up, blow-ing sand into the fugitive's tracks and obliterating them. By noon the winds had reached gale proportions, whipping up a stinging sand blizzard.

The Papagos, who knew the desert well, decided to abandon the chase. Putting the storm at their backs they headed north toward Quitobaquito. A short time later, as the posse struggled over a particularly large dune, the wind suddenly died. Then, as they crossed over the dune, they saw through the haze the belfry of the Mission of the Four Evangelists. It jutted up from the desert floor near the bottom of the next dune. The Indians did not pause. They all knew the story of the lost mission, but they also knew that the lull in the wind could be temporary, and their primary concern was to get out of the desert.

Upon their return to the Colorado River camp, however, they told of their discovery, and word eventually reached a priest named Father Paul Kelley in Yuma. The priest went to their camp and attempted to enlist an expedition to take him to the site. He abandoned the project, however, after the Indians convinced him that the mission would have once again sunk beneath the desert sands.

The story of the lost mission is best told by the Papagos:

Many years ago there had been a large oasis at the site. It had been protected for centuries by small mountains that rose to a low elevation on three sides of it. There was a spring in the center of this oasis which the Papagos called Open Jaw, and the area was extensive enough to support a village of more than five hundred Papagos.

Then the Spanish arrived, including a detachment of soldiers and about a dozen priests. The strangers were made welcome. The soldiers dug in the earth of the mountain and found traces of gold, enough so that when the detachment moved on, they left behind two priests and a half-dozen soldiers. The priests taught the Papagos a new religion, how to make adobe bricks from the earth of the mountain, and how to dig out the gold. The soldiers devoted their time to making sure that the Indians were attentive pupils.

From the moment of the strangers' arrival, however, trouble seemed to appear in the village. The level of the spring became lower, and three years passed without a drop of rain. Some of the Indians attempted to explain to the priests that they were using too much water in their placer mining (a process by which water is used to separate the heavier particles of gold from the lighter gravel), but the padres would not listen or did not understand. The mining continued and a church was built. Two more priests arrived on the day the church was completed, and they brought with them a small bell that was hung in the belfry of the new building. At first the new church was called the Mission of the Four Padres, but a short time later was changed to the Mission of the Four Evangelists.

As the drought continued, the mountains, which were nothing more than huge piles of gold-bearing dirt, began to erode. At the same time the spring became so low that there was not enough water to support the village and the mining. Gradually the Papagos began to slip away, heading for other villages. Then the sand from the desert began to blow in on the oasis. The mining stopped. Two of the priests left, leaving behind only six soldiers to guard the other two.

One morning the remaining Papagos awoke to find the priests, the soldiers, and two more members of their village gone. Also missing was a large amount of gold that had been stored in the church. The Indians gathered together and worked themselves into a collective rage. The Spaniards had been welcomed upon their arrival. The Papagos had accepted their religion, their authority, and had worked as slaves in their mines. In return their village had been destroyed, and they had been deserted. The Spaniards even had taken gold, which rightfully belonged to the Papagos.

Before the day was warm, the men of the village were on the warpath and in full pursuit of the Spaniards. They were more fortunate than their descendants who chased a prospector over the same route a few centuries later. The war party caught up with the fleeing Spaniards before noon. In the first skirmish the two Papagos, who had been impressed as porters to carry the gold, were killed. The Spanish paused long enough to bury the two Indians, then resumed their flight. About an hour later the Papagos attacked again. The two priests and one of the soldiers were killed in this attack. Before nightfall the Indians had killed all of the Spaniards.

When no trace of the gold could be found, the Papagos understood why the Spaniards had paused long enough to bury two Indians while the other bodies were abandoned where they fell. They knew the Spaniards were well aware of the Papago superstition that to disturb an Indian's grave is to bring down a curse of death. The perfect way to cache the gold until it could be recovered would be to leave it guarded by two Indian spirits. The gold surely had been placed in the grave before the corpses of the dead Indians.

The most recent known search for the Mission of the Four Evangelists was undertaken in 1964 by the Arizona adventurer John Powell. Alone and on foot, he traveled the desolate route from El Doctor to Camino del Diablo.

He estimated that his trip would take two days. On the evening of the first day he made camp at the base of one of the sand mountains that hide the mission and Laguna Prieta. Writing of his experiences later in *Desert* magazine, Powell described his surroundings as "a silent, yellow sea of sand, billowing endlessly, and void of all life and movement." In the morning he found a fragment of a pottery olla, a clay water vessel, but the heat was too intense for him to linger in the area. He was virtually exhausted by the time he stumbled onto the paved highway after dark on the second evening where he was picked up by a friend. Later, he guessed that he had missed his projected route through the Gran Desierto by approximately twenty miles.

There is another version of the legend of the lost Mission of the Four Evangelists, an account that is accepted more easily on the northern than on the southern side of the United States-Mexico border. This tells the story of Don Padriac Odonoju, which is a loose Spanish interpretation of the name Patrick O'Donahue.

O'Donahue joined the Spanish in fighting the British in various naval encounters during the late seventeenth century. He was rewarded for his endeavors by the King of Spain with a Spanish name and a land grant in Papagueria, an area now known as the Altar Valley in southern Arizona. Although the grant of more than twelve leagues was in one of the most desolate areas of the Spanish New World, Don Padriac liked his new title and his surroundings.

He called his vast hacienda "The Garden of Solitude," and the mission he built near his ornate living quarters was called the "Mission of the Four Evangelists." Both the mission and Don Padriac's house were covered with gold mined by the Papagos in the nearby Baboquivari Range. Additionally, a fortune in gold bars was stored in the hacienda.

The end of Don Padriac's prosperous existence came suddenly one morning shortly before dawn. A band of Apaches descended upon the hacienda, killing everyone from the lowest Papago servant to Don Padriac. They left, taking only the horses, other livestock, and brightly colored cloths. They had no use for the gold.

Because of their superstition of the dead, other Papagos shunned the Garden of Solitude and over the years it gradually became engulfed by the "walking" sands.

The Mission of the Four Evangelists will be bared again briefly, be it on the shores of Laguna Prieta or in the Altar Valley. In either case, somewhere nearby will be the spirits of dead Papagos guarding a fortune in gold.

THE MURDER OF LEVI MACGRUDER

Hill Beachy was something of an enigma to his many friends in Lewiston, Idaho. To begin with, his name was considered strange. There were some who thought it was an assumed name, for Hill Beachy, like many other residents of the West in the mid-nineteenth century, was vague about his past. He arrived in Lewiston about 1860, when he was in his early thirties. He built a hotel in the booming town, which at that time was the closest supply center to the gold camps. At first he was considered a fop because of his elegant dress. Even in the mornings he would wear clean, white, starched shirts, and he owned enough suits to wear a different one each day for two months before repeating his attire.

The service in his hotel was superb. Bed linens were changed daily, even for semipermanent guests, and the cuisine in his dining room was the finest to be found between San Francisco and Chicago.

Hill Beachy established himself as a leading citizen in Lewiston when he faced two gunmen in the saloon he owned adjacent to his hotel. No one could recall what started the dispute, but for approximately a quarter of an hour two hoodlums confronted each other at the bar with guns pointed at each other's midriff. The saloon emptied and one of the fleeing patrons ran to Hill Beachy with the news.

The proprietor rose from his desk and strode into the saloon, walking directly over to the two men. "I do not tolerate this kind of behavior in my place of business," he said quietly. "You both shall leave immediately."

"Listen to the dandy," one of the gunman said belligerently.

The bartender said later that Hill Beachy moved so quickly that for a second he was invisible. During that one second, the gunman who had sneered at Hill Beachy landed on the floor of the tavern with a broken arm and the gun he had been holding was in the clenched fist of the hotel proprietor. "Out," Hill Beachy told the other gunman. The man did not move. A split second later his gun went flying from his hand as Hill Beachy put a bullet in his arm. Hill Beachy then suggested for the second time that both men leave, a suggestion they followed with alacrity.

When word of this incident spread around Lewiston, Hill Beachy was shifted to another category. Instead of being thought of as the peculiar dandy who owned the hotel, he now was considered a prominent citizen of the community who certainly was entitled to his few eccentricities. Had he so wanted, he could have been elected mayor, a member of the town council, or sheriff, but Hill Beachy wanted nothing other

141

than to operate his hotel. And this he did unobtrusively until 1863, when he took off on a six-month manhunt that would strain the imagination of even the most inventive Western Americana buff.

Hill Beachy's closest friend in Lewiston was Levi Mac-Gruder, a wealthy young trader who probably collected more gold from the camps in Idaho and Montana than many of the miners who worked them. MacGruder was married, but it is not known whether he had any children. When he was in town, many of his evenings were spent playing chess with Hill Beachy in the lobby of the hotel. The only place Hill Beachy would eat outside of his hotel was in MacGruder's home, and more often than not the finicky Beachy would arrive accompanied by a hotel busboy carrying dinner.

MacGruder's trading trips often involved excursions lasting more than three or four months. Early on the morning of August 3, 1863, MacGruder left Lewiston with a pack train of one hundred mules. His destination was Virginia City, Montana, more than 300 miles away, but his route there was not a direct one. He planned to trace a twisted path, hitting scores of mining camps between the two cities. As usual on these midsummer trips he was shorthanded. Mule skinners were hard to find when the weather was good, and they had been lured away by tales of new strikes in gold and silver.

MacGruder had been gone about two weeks when Hill Beachy received a letter from him, brought back to Lewiston by stagecoach. He wrote that he had been fortunate. On the third day out of Lewiston, his slow-moving train had been overtaken by a group of eight horsemen. One of them was Bill Page, a trapper and a scout known by MacGruder for a long time. He identified three others in the group as Jim Romaine, Dan Lowry, and Dave Howard, all who claimed to be from Lewiston, but who were strangers to MacGruder. The men agreed to sign on the train as mule skinners until they reached Virginia City.

Hill Beachy received another letter from his friend around the first of October. This trip, he said, had been one of the most profitable he had ever undertaken. He had collected more than $30,000 in gold dust and an additional $20,000 in gold coins. Romaine, Lowry, Page, and Howard, along with his regular four mule skinners were returning to Lewiston with the pack train. He anticipated that the journey would be of short duration, providing the snows held off.

October passed the halfway mark and MacGruder had not arrived. There had been a fall blizzard that had delayed the stage for a couple of days, but this would not have delayed MacGruder for much more than the same length of time. Even if he had only averaged thirty miles a day, his arrival was seriously overdue. Hill Beachy saddled up his horse and went looking.

He assumed that MacGruder would follow the stage trail on his return trip, and so Hill Beachy followed this route to Virginia City. At each stage stop he inquired after his friend. Most of the operators at each depot knew MacGruder. Hill Beachy could not find one stage operator in Idaho who had seen the pack train on its return trip until he got high up in the Bitter Root Mountains. Here the proprietor of the stage stop was positive that Levi MacGruder had passed early in October. Hill Beachy narrowed his search between the two stage depots, the one where his friend had been seen and the one he had failed to pass. He found no trace of MacGruder. A lot of snow had fallen in the mountains, covering any clues that might have explained his friend's mysterious disappearance.

Reluctantly Hill Beachy returned to Lewiston. He was puzzled as well as worried. One hundred mules, nine horses, and nine men simply could not vanish without some explanation. If they had been ambushed by Indians, there surely would have been signs of the massacre remaining, which would have been seen by a passing stage. Besides, if the train had been attacked by Indians, MacGruder would have fought, and his men and mules would have scattered. MacGruder was carrying $50,000 in gold. Hill Beachy could not shake this thought.

A break in the mystery came about a week after Hill Beachy's return. A groom who worked in the livery stable that served the hotel guests came to see Hill Beachy in an excited state. "That man who just checked into the hotel is riding Mr. MacGruder's horse," he said.

MacGruder rode a large paint, distinctive because an almost exact copy of the map of Italy was etched in white along one side of the animal. The horse naturally was named Italy and, a short time later when Hill Beachy arrived in the stables, he responded to his name.

The stranger was in the dining room when Hill Beachy returned to the hotel. As the man had just started his dinner, Hill Beachy thought it a good time to search the man's room. He discovered that the man riding MacGruder's horse was a Methodist circuit rider from Boise. Hill Beachy sighed, returned to the dining room, and sat down across from the new arrival.

The traveling minister was nonplused. "I bought that horse from a livery in Walla Walla, Washington, about three weeks ago. I have a bill of sale."

The bill of sale appeared legitimate and Hill Beachy thought it unlikely that a man of the cloth had had anything to do with MacGruder's disappearance. The minister could

144

tell him nothing more than that Italy was one of several horses the livery stable had had up for sale. Before the dinner was finished, the circuit rider no longer owned Italy. He had sold him, at a considerable profit, to Hill Beachy.

The following day Hill Beachy left Lewiston for Walla Walla, riding Italy. The livery-stable operator remembered the paint well. The horse was one of four animals he had purchased from four men early in October. The quartet had said they were miners who had struck it rich and were heading back home. The stable operator had not bothered to inquire where "home" was, but he had insisted upon a bill of sale for the animals. The bills of sale were signed respectively by William Page, D. C. Lowry, David Howard, and James Romaine.

"Did they buy any other horses?" Hill Beachy asked.

"Nope."

"Have you seen them around town?"

"Nope."

Hill Beachy went to the stage company. The four men had departed from Walla Walla by stage for Portland, Oregon, on October 14. He remained overnight in Walla Walla, writing several letters. One went to the sheriff in Lewiston asking that a warrant for the arrest of the four men be sent on to him in Portland. He also wrote to the governors of Washington, Oregon, and California, disingenuously identifying himself as a deputy sheriff and asking that the quartet be "requisitioned" for trial in Lewiston. In none of the letters did he mention a criminal act for which the men reportedly were under suspicion. The next morning, still riding Italy, Hill Beachy set out for Portland.

It was a long and cold journey, but Hill Beachy did not pause to rest once he had arrived in Portland. He picked up the trail immediately. Lowry, Howard, and Romaine had been big spenders while they were in the city. Page had been around, but had spent most of his time in the hotel room. He discovered that all four men had been booked on a coastal steamer for San Francisco, but only Page had shown up. At first Page had boarded the steamer, but then cancelled his passage a few minutes before the vessel sailed. His companions had missed the boat because they were drunk. Ten days before Hill Beachy's arrival in the river-port city, the four men had embarked on another coastal steamer for San Francisco.

Another steamer was not due in Portland for three weeks. Hill Beachy saddled up Italy and took off for San Francisco. The records do not report how long it took him to make the long and arduous trip to the city by the Golden Gate. It is known, however, that when he reached Yreka, not far from the Oregon border in California, he discovered there was a telegraphic link between Yreka and San Francisco. Again, identifying himself as a deputy sheriff, he wired the San Francisco police a description of the four men, which he had picked up in Walla Walla and Portland, along with a request that they be taken into custody. The San Francisco Police Department decided it needed something a little more authentic before launching a search.

When Hill Beachy arrived in San Francisco, the police were still reluctant to cooperate. He was accused of impersonating a peace officer, but no action was taken against him. The San Francisco police agreed to write to the police in Lewiston for confirmation that the four men sought by Hill Beachy were indeed fugitives. Hill Beachy wisely refrained from telling the San Francisco police that all the information the Lewiston sheriff had also came from him.

At this time, San Francisco was already a large city by

western standards. There were dozens of hotels and hundreds of boardinghouses in the city, any one of which could house his quarry. The arrival of four more free-spending miners would go unnoticed since the Barbary Coast was full of them.

Hill Beachy, however, was not a man to be easily discouraged. He started with the best hotel, the Palace, and learned that the four men had spent five days there, immediately after their arrival in the city. When they moved on, they had left no forwarding address. He scoured the hotels of the city. Two weeks later, Hill Beachy found William Page. He was living in a small hotel on lower California Street.

The encounter was not a dramatic one. When Hill Beachy asked at the desk for the four men by name, the clerk pointed to a man with an emaciated look sitting in one of the chairs in the lobby. "That's Page," the clerk said. "I don't have the others."

Page seemed relieved when Hill Beachy went over and quietly introduced himself. He told his story to the confidence-inviting hotelier in the lobby of the hotel. He had met his three companions about two weeks before they ran into Mac-Gruder, who had just left Lewiston. All of them were amazed at the hoard of gold MacGruder accumulated as he sold off his wares and supplies. They originally had planned to travel with the mule train only as far as Virginia City. Shortly before they arrived, Page overheard Lowry and Romaine making plans to rob MacGruder. He was caught eavesdropping and was given the choice of participating in the robbery or being killed. Page decided that participation was the lesser of two evils. The four men then volunteered to continue on as mule skinners on the return trip to Lewiston, an offer which Mac-Gruder accepted gratefully.

The night it was Page's turn to stand guard was chosen

as the time for the attack. Lowry killed MacGruder as he slept, striking him on the head with an axe. Romaine and Howard then slaughtered the four regular mule skinners in a similar fashion. One mule was selected to carry provisions and the gold. The other mules and extra horses were then driven over a high cliff into a deep ravine to their death. The bodies of the victims were tossed off the cliff along with the superfluous camping gear.

"How much of the money is left?"

Page shook his head. He had been given only $5,000 as his share. The $20,000 in gold coins was buried at the base of a bluff beside the stagecoach road about a day's ride out of Walla Walla. This had been Lowry's idea. By posing as miners, they could justify the possession of gold dust. But if the bodies were found immediately with the coins still in the bandits' possession, they would be automatically suspect, Lowry suggested, and his two friends agreed. Page added that he believed Lowry planned to return alone and pick up the gold coins.

The former trapper and scout seemed eager to accompany Hill Beachy to police headquarters and tell his story. This time the police listened. Later the same evening the police located Howard, Lowry, and Romaine and arrested them.

It is not known how the four murderers were returned to Lewiston. It is known, however, that they arrived on Christmas Eve, 1863, were tried the following month, and all except Page were hanged on March 4. Page was freed after he testified for the prosecution.

In May, a little more than two months after the triple execution, the snows had melted sufficiently to expose the bodies of the massacre victims and support the story told by

148

Page. The gold dust that was recovered from the highwaymen was given to MacGruder's widow. In June, Hill Beachy accompanied Page to the area where the $20,000 in gold coins had been buried. It was a futile trip. There were too many bluffs, and Page was confused. The former trapper died in Lewiston the following August.

Hill Beachy's efforts did not go unrewarded. The territorial legislature appropriated $6,244 to be paid to Hill Beachy as reimbursement for expenses incurred during his long pursuit of his friend's murderers.

The $20,000 in gold coins remains secreted at the base of a bluff on the old stage trail between Walla Walla, Washington, and Lewiston, Idaho, about a day's ride by horse outside the old city limits of Walla Walla.

THE LOST CABIN NUGGETS

One of the most spectacular and forbidding strings of mountain peaks in the United States is the Wind River Range in the northwest corner of the thinly populated state of Wyoming. The range of snow-capped peaks continues in a southeasterly direction from Yellowstone National Park and is adjacent to the more publicized Grand Tetons of Jackson Hole. Vast areas of the Wind River Range have never been explored by white men even though gold was discovered in this area more than seven years before the strike at Sutter's Creek triggered the gold rush to California.

Gold was first found in these mountains by a trapper from Georgia. His name has been lost in history, but the story most commonly told about him proves that he was not a greedy man. When he struck gold, he gathered up as many nuggets as he could carry and, with winter approaching, set out for the warmer clime of his native state. As he had no plans of ever returning to Wyoming, he made no secret of where he had found his gold. He was, however, rather vague in his directions, not intentionally, but because he had paid no attention to landmarks on his way out of the mountains.

He cashed in two of his nuggets in Fort Laramie, telling anyone interested where he had found them. By morning of the next day, a party of forty prospectors had been organized and was en route to the area. The following day, the commanding officer of the fort learned of the exodus and, for reasons never made public, sent a detachment of soldiers after the prospectors. The military confiscated all of the miners' equipment and forced them all back to Fort Laramie.

Many years later two of these prospectors who by then were semiretired told a young adventurer named Allan Hurlburt from Walla Walla, Washington, about their experiences. The tale of the homesick Georgian laden with nuggets, and the subsequent confrontation with the military intrigued Hurlburt. He pumped the two oldtimers for all the information they had. He then convinced two friends, Freitag and Smith, to accompany him on a search of the remote Wind River Range for the spot where gold nuggets were strewn around the ground like a sea of pebbles. His friends did not need much to convince them. Tales of fabulous lodes of gold around South Pass City had already reached Walla Walla. South Pass City now had a population of more than four thousand, despite the plethora of hostile Indians in the area. The Wind River Range was just to the west of South Pass City. With no more then these facts to go on, the heavily armed trio set out for what was then Dakota Territory.

The trip to South Pass City was uneventful. When they arrived, with the prospectors' customary reticence they indicated that they planned to look around the Sweetwater Range some miles to the east. They purchased three pack mules and enough supplies to last for several months.

For weeks they traveled up and down the sides of the mountains and through the steep canyons. Game was plentiful and even the sound of rifle shots failed to attract the attention of any hostile Indians. In late August they camped one night beside a small, swift-running stream. As Hurlburt bent over to scoop up some water for coffee, something flashed in the bottom of the stream. A moment later he had recovered a huge nugget of pure gold. The nuggets were not lying around like a sea of pebbles but, within the next hour, the three men found more than a dozen nuggets in the streambed. They obviously had been washed down from an extraordinarily rich vein higher up in the mountains.

For the next several days the men worked the stream on a share-and-share-alike principle, each night dividing the day's take as nearly as possible into three equal parts. After a little more than a week, however, the stream had been cleared of nuggets. Using the camping spot as a base, the three prospectors began working their way farther upstream, searching for the lode.

One night upon their return, they discovered that the gate to the corral was broken, and the mules and horses had disappeared. Hurlburt found bear tracks near the edge of the stream and the three men decided the horses had panicked at the sight of the bear and had crashed open the gate of the flimsy corral. Hurlburt thought it strange, however, that the bear had not gotten into the supplies and that the horses had not returned for feed, since there was little in the way of pasture in the area.

About the middle of September, they found the vein of

gold. It was a streak so pure that it did not need refining. The three men could pack enough out to become multimillionaires. First, however, they had to dig it out, which would take months, and, second, they would need some mules on which they could transport it. A decision was reached. They had plenty of ammunition, game was plentiful, and they were not low on supplies. It would be pointless to leave their discovery and come back to it. They decided to build a cabin in the wide spot by the stream where Hurlburt had found the first nugget. After the cabin was built they would work on the mine until forced to stop by cold or snow. The winter would be spent in the cabin. Come spring, one of the three would go to South Pass City to buy some more mules and horses.

It did not take long to build a log cabin. They even built a fireplace for heat and cooking during the winter. Hurlburt was finishing work on the cabin one chilly day in early October while Freitag and Smith went up to the mine to start work on the excavation. About noon, Hurlburt heard the sound of rifle shots in the distance. They came from the direction of the mine, but Hurlburt was not alarmed. He thought his partners probably were shooting at a wild animal.

He did become alarmed, however, when night fell, and Freitag and Smith failed to return. Leaving the cabin, he climbed up to the mine in the dark. He called out the names of his partners, but there was no answer. There was no possibility of a mine accident, since the shaft had not been excavated to a depth of more than five or six feet. He finally returned to his cabin.

The following morning he again returned to the lode site and in the light of day saw that the ground around the shaft was stained with blood. A short time later he found Smith's body, stripped of its outer clothing and thrown into some brush. As he bent over the body some atavistic sense told him that he was being watched, that he was in danger. He dove over the body of his dead partner and a split second later heard a rifle shot. A bullet ricocheted from a rock in front of him.

Hurlburt rolled down the hill behind Smith's body, narrowly escaping the gunman's bullets. A moment later he reached the sanctuary of a huge boulder. He still held his rifle. After half an hour, he heard footsteps slithering down the shale of the hill. He did not consider himself a heroic man, but he was intelligent enough to know that if he did nothing, he would soon be slaughtered like his partner. He stood up and fired. The force of the bullet threw an Indian flat on his back less than fifty feet away.

The Indian was alone. He wore Smith's pants and carried Smith's rifle. Hurlburt paused only long enough to pick up his partner's rifle, then took a long circuituous route back to the cabin. He planned to stay at the cabin only long enough to pick up as many of the nuggets as he could carry and enough grub to last for the long trek to South Pass City. He knew it was improbable that the dead Indian had traveled alone, but he hoped that the other Indians had not yet discovered the cabin. Hurlburt made a wide circle around the campsite, then approached it stealthily from below.

His hopes were in vain. He heard the Indians before he saw them; a half-dozen were gathered in the clearing. During the time he had made his long circular trip back to the cabin, they had retrieved the body of their companion whom Hurlburt had shot at the mine. They were now wrapping the body in Hurlburt's bedroll, probably preparing to take it back to their village for burial. An unpleasant thought occurred to

154

Hurlburt. Some Indians could well be behind him, having followed his trail from the site of the killing. He thought of the nuggets buried under the dirt floor of the cabin. Before they had buried the nuggets, he and his partners had estimated their worth to be about $30,000 a share. The thought flickered through Hurlburt's mind that with his partners dead, the $90,000 worth of gold was all his. But his life was invaluable. The Indians might watch the cabin for days, expecting him to return. The Indians were not interested in gold, and even if by some slight chance they were, they would know nothing of the nuggets found in the creek bed.

Hurlburt left.

A little more than a month later, a merchant traveling between Miners Delight and Atlantic City, Wyoming, came across a gaunt man staggering along the road. The man could not talk intelligibly, but the merchant took him into Atlantic City where he was treated by a physician for malnutrition and frostbite. The man, of course, was Hurlburt, and by the time he had recovered sufficiently to tell his story, the snows were too deep for him to return to the mountains. Hurlburt had no idea of the route he had taken to get out. Very early in his flight he had discarded Smith's rifle. On the second or third day he had fallen, and his own rifle had slipped from his grasp and disappeared over the side of a steep cliff. He had been caught in two blizzards and chilling cold. He knew that if he stopped moving he would die. He ate snow and bark. Once he killed a porcupine with a rock and carried the carcass with him, eating it slowly for days.

When he had recovered, Hurlburt went home to Walla Walla to spend the winter. The following June he returned to South Pass City. By then the story he had told while delirious in Atlantic City was known in South Pass City, too. Three men followed Hurlburt's trail into the Wind River Range, but Hurlburt was able to shake them.

Early in September Hurlburt once again came out of the mountains. He carried Smith's rusted rifle, which he had found by accident. He had been unable to find the stream or the abandoned log cabin. He tried to enlist some men in South Pass City to go back into the mountains with him, but was unable to organize a group because of the rapidly approaching winter storms.

Hurlburt returned to South Pass City again the following spring. This time he had little difficulty attracting help and, in late April, Hurlburt and four other men once more entered the Wind River Range. During the ensuing months the search party came across several streams, which they followed as closely as possible to their source. None flowed by the former campsite. The cabin, or the ruins of the cabin, could not be found. In August Hurlburt abruptly gave up the search, went back to Walla Walla, and never again returned to Wyoming.

A year later, a prospector named Joe Poole came down from the Wind River Range. He had found the skeleton of a white man who had been shot in the head, he told patrons of a South Pass City tavern.

"How do you know it was a white man?" he was asked.

"Because he had boots on and there was a leather belt around where his belly had been."

It was unlikely that there was anyone in the bar who by then had not heard of Hurlburt's lost nuggets and his experience. The prospector was asked if there was a small stream near the skeleton.

"Yep, there was," Poole replied.

"How about a log cabin. Did you see a log cabin?"

156

Poole had not seen a cabin, but he was confident that he could find the skeleton. It would take about four or five days to reach it. More than a dozen citizens of South Pass City followed Joe Poole into the Wind River Range on the following day. Poole's confidence had been excessive. For more than two weeks he led the group up and down the canyons looking in vain for the skeleton.

The cabin remained lost for about twenty years. Then, shortly after the turn of the nineteenth century, another prospector named J. H. Osborne showed up in South Pass City after the conclusion of a prospecting trip in the Wind River Range. He had in his possession three large gold nuggets. He had found them in a stream, he said, and had spent weeks looking for a lode in the area, but had been unable to find one. If there were any more nuggets in the creek, he had been unable to find them either. Someone else had been there before him because there were the ruins of a log cabin nearby.

Osborne had drifted on before his story reached anyone who recalled Hurlburt.

South Pass City today is almost a ghost town a few miles south of Lander. Some people still live there and many of the buildings still stand. There no longer are hostile Indians in the Wind River Range, but the winters can be severe. It is unlikely that anything remains today of Hurlburt's log cabin other than the stones from a fireplace. But if someone happened across the remnants of a fireplace facing a stream in a cleared area, he could well dig up a fortune in gold nuggets.

TECHATTICUP GOLD

Between Las Vegas and Searchlight in Nevada is the small ghost town of Nelson. It can be reached easily by car. It was a town supported by two mines from which millions of dollars' worth of gold was taken and in which millions more is believed to remain. According to the old-timers still living in the area, the two mines were not shut down because of economic factors, but they were abandoned because they were cursed. There were few mining camps in the West that did not have a high incidence of violent deaths, but few can match Nelson for its record of conspiratorial murder and devious theft.

One of the mines is the Techatticup which, in Paiute Indian dialect, means "plenty for all." The other is referred to by some as the Queen City Mine. Others call it the Savage Mine.

The Techatticup is the older mine, its first shaft dug by Spanish explorers. The ore was nearly pure gold. The first pack train of ore started out for Mexico City in 1703, but before the caravan reached the shores of the Colorado River a few miles away, it was attacked by a horde of Paiutes. Its cargo of nuggets was strewn on the ground. About half of

158

the soldiers escorting the pack train escaped and most of them carried samples of the golden cargo with them. Many also drew maps of the area that were accurate enough to lead a more heavily armed detachment back to the mine the following year.

As soon as the mine was located, soldiers raided several Indian villages for the necessary slave labor to operate it. The Indians retaliated with such ferocity that the Spanish were forced to abandon the venture. Most of the Spaniards were killed but, once again, a few arrived back in Mexico City carrying nuggets, which gave substance to the tales of the fabulous wealth of the Techatticup. With two expeditionary forces to the area virtually wiped out, the Spanish were reluctant to send a third detachment into the hostile area. However, the maps describing the location of the mine were kept in the archives, and, approximately three-quarters of a century later, another group of Spanish soldiers and explorers were sent to the mine.

The Indians had long memories, and they still wanted no part of the white race digging up the land. This massacre was a carbon copy of the first. The Paiutes waited until the first pack train had departed for Mexico, then ambushed it a few miles from the camp. Again the ore and nuggets were scattered on the ground, the members of the caravan slaughtered, and the animals confiscated. The Paiutes then descended upon those who had remained in the camp and killed everyone there.

The Spanish gave up on the project. The maps describing the location remained scattered in profusion around Mexico. Around 1840 a prospector named Jack Nelson acquired one of these maps from a Mexican in El Paso. It was so accurate that it led him directly to the Techatticup, and Nelson was able to load up his pack mule with nuggets and ore and get back to El Paso without attracting the attention of the Paiutes. Legend says that the most surprised person to see Nelson return with the ore was the Mexican who had sold him the map.

Word of Nelson's "strike" spread like fire, and within weeks the hills around the Techatticup were swarming with prospectors. The Paiutes welcomed this invasion with the same enthusiasm they had accorded the Spaniards. One of the first men to fall victim to the Paiutes was Nelson. The fatalities were high on both sides, but there were too many white men this time for the Indians to wipe out. A combine was formed to operate the Techatticup, and the operation was so well guarded that the Indians suffered fearsome losses during the three occasions when they attacked. Soldiers were brought in to protect the property. The gold ore was taken out by steamboats that sailed up the Colorado River to El Dorado Canyon from Yuma, a voyage of more than three hundred and fifty miles. Supplies were brought in the same vessels, successfully blocking the Paiute habit of raiding pack trains.

A quarter of a century after Nelson's discovery, the Techatticup Mine was still living up to its name, "plenty for all." Another mine adjoining it, the Queen City, was equally productive and had been purchased by George Hearst, father of William Randolph Hearst, the newspaper mogul.

Then, around 1865, John Nash arrived in the town of Nelson. Nash came from San Francisco where he had organized the Eldorado Mining Company, which had purchased the Techatticup Mine. Little is known about Nash's background. He was a large man, close-shaven, and usually soft-spoken. He also was dangerous and dishonest.

One day, a few weeks after Nash had taken over operation of the Techatticup, a young man arrived on the river steamer and asked for directions to Nash's house. He was seen going into the house. His body was found a couple of days later on the outskirts of town. Nash blandly denied that he knew the youth and that he ever had seen him, suggesting that the victim was probably a drifter slain by the Indians. Because Nash, through his position as owner of the Techatticup, was above what little law existed in the area, no one seriously questioned his story.

About a year later, another visitor arrived on the steamer and asked for directions to Nash's house. Moments after he entered the dwelling, there was the sound of a gunshot.

"The man is an absolute stranger," Nash said, pointing with his gun toward the body of the stranger lying on the floor. "He started to attack me and I shot him in self-defense."

There were some who said the stranger had been unarmed, and many thought it odd that a man should travel with no identification on his person, but no one bothered Nash.

For reasons probably known only to himself, George Hearst did not operate the Queen City Mine. To protect his claim, Hearst sent in a small crew once a year for development work. Nash coveted the Queen City Mine, and in 1872 an opportunity arose for him to grab it. Only three weeks remained before a full year would have passed since Hearst's agents had appeared for their token development work.

Nash hired three of the toughest thugs he could find to jump the claim, promising to pay each of them $10,000 for holding the property for only three weeks. The leader of this trio was a man named Ray Wareman. The other two were William Pirtle and Jim Jones.

About two weeks after the three had taken possession of the Queen City Mine, Hearst's agents arrived on the river steamer. When they approached their property, bullets whistled over their heads. There were no lawmen to turn to for help, so the agents returned to the steamer and sailed back to Yuma. When word of what happened got back to Hearst, he immediately filed suit in the courts against the "three John Does" who had jumped his Queen City Mine claim. He was much too late. The day after the year ended, the Eldorado Mining Company claimed title to the Queen City Mine, contending that it had been abandoned because no development work had been done on the property during the past year. Nash did not even bother to wait for the issue to be decided by the court. He immediately started working the Queen City.

Wareman, the most dangerous of the three hoods, was paid his $10,000 immediately and left the area. Nash decided on a less costly maneuver to dispose of Pirtle and Jones. He promised to pay Pirtle the entire $20,000 if he would get rid of Jones. Accordingly, Pirtle shot Jones in the back a few mornings later as Jones was bent over a wash basin. The wound was not fatal. Jones grabbed his rifle and killed Pirtle.

Nash expressed shock when he heard about the shooting. "It's time we had some law and order in this community," he said. "Jim Jones should be tried for murder."

One of Nash's men was appointed a town marshal, and he went to Jones's cabin to arrest him. The new town marshal's tenure was extraordinarily short. He was killed when he tried to take Jones from his cabin. Jones apparently decided that his future in the community was bleak, for, despite his wound, he fled. Nash was still not satisfied. "We must have justice," he said. "Cold-blooded murder can no longer be tolerated here."

A posse was formed. By late afternoon, the posse had trapped Jones in a small cave near the bank of the Colorado

River. Before night fell, Jones had killed one member of the posse and wounded another. The group fell back, but kept Jones pinned in the cave during the night. The following morning Nash appeared. "I will talk to him and see if I can get him to surrender," he said. He rode up to the mouth of the cave, calling out his own name as he went. "It's all right, Jim," he was heard to say. "You can come out now."

A moment later Jim Jones lurched out of his sanctuary. He was holding his rifle loosely in one hand, the muzzle pointed toward the ground. Nash waited until Jones was almost abreast of him. Then he whipped out his revolver and shot his former employee twice in the head.

By his action, Nash had successfully eliminated his conspirators in the acquisition of the Queen City Mine, but he probably did not realize that his murder of Jones would alienate him in the community. This town of outlaws and miners had its own peculiar code of ethics. Shooting a man down while he was surrendering was not considered fair play. A day or so later, when Nash was inspecting his newly acquired Queen City Mine, someone shot at him. His horse was killed, but Nash escaped uninjured. A week later someone fired another shot in his direction as he was entering his house.

The second attack apparently frightened Nash more than the first. He left on the next steamer for Yuma, and when he returned he was accompanied by two men. One he introduced as his brother-in-law, Bill Davis, although Nash had never indicated that he was married or that he had any brothers or sisters. The second stranger was William Piette, whose basic function was that of bodyguard. A few weeks later, a third man arrived and moved into the Nash home. His last name was Fuller. His first name has been lost in time.

Both Fuller and Davis were experienced mining men, and

163

for a while they concentrated their efforts on getting the Queen City Mine into operation. Fuller, however, had an incurable case of prospecting fever. Late in 1873, about a year after his arrival, Fuller found an incredibly rich lode of gold about six miles from the Techatticup Mine. He named his discovery the Bridal Chamber, and not only quit working for Nash, but persuaded Davis to do so and join him as a partner in the Bridal Chamber.

The first shipment of the almost pure ore from the Bridal Chamber shipped by pack mule to the riverfront was hijacked. Davis, accompanying the mules, made no secret of his belief that John Nash was responsible. There are two versions of what happened next. One states that Davis went to see Nash at his home, was welcomed cordially and was invited to have dinner with Piette and Nash. During the dinner, Nash denied any complicity in the hijack, and he offered to buy back the shares that Davis held in the Eldorado Mining Company. Davis agreed to sell his holdings for cash, which Nash gave him.

A few minutes after his departure from Nash's house, Davis fell from his horse, his body twisting convulsively. Piette rushed from the house and carried Davis back inside, then raced into town to summon the town's doctor. Before he arrived, however, Davis was dead. The doctor reported that there were many indications that Davis had been poisoned.

The other version of the story contends that Piette met Davis in a saloon where, acting as Nash's agent, the same deal was agreed upon over the disposition of Davis's stock in the Eldorado Mining Company. This version has Davis collapsing in the saloon a few minutes after the deal was consummated.

Both stories relate that the money Davis was paid disappeared before his body arrived at the town's undertaker and that Piette was the first man at Davis's side when he collapsed.

A few days after Davis was buried, Piette journeyed up into the mountains to see Fuller. It was June, the time of year when the waters of the Colorado were near flood stage, and, when Piette arrived, Fuller was directing a crew of Indians in snagging driftwood to store up for fuel. The wife of one of the crew was in Fuller's cabin when Piette rode up. She ran to fetch Fuller.

The miner angrily ordered Piette from his property, and the bodyguard rode off without a word. That night, while eating his dinner, Fuller was seized by convulsions and died within a quarter-hour. His body was buried near the cabin. A day or so later Nash and Piette arrived and formally claimed possession of the Bridal Chamber.

There was little doubt in the minds of all in the area that Davis and Fuller were poisoned by Piette at Nash's instigation. Several accounts of the apparent double murder even identify the poison as strychnine. Once again, the ethics of the western mining camps were violated. Killing by gunfire was understandable, but poisoning was considered the coward's murder method.

Nash's fate probably will be a mystery forever. He simply disappeared. He did not leave the mining camp. Piette reported that he went to bed leaving Nash sipping a whiskey. When Piette arose in the morning, Nash was gone. There was no steamer at the riverbank. Nash's horses were still in the stable and his personal possessions remained in his home. But there was never again any sign of John Nash himself. Many weeks after he disappeared, a man claiming to represent the Eldorado Mining Company arrived on the supply steamer. He found all three of the mines shut down. The miners would not work without pay and most of them had drifted on. Piette still lived in Nash's house, but did not appear to need funds. The stranger made no attempt to get the mines back in operation. Instead he boarded up the shafts, searched Nash's house thoroughly, and then departed with a suitcase full of papers Nash had left behind.

A few months later, Piette entered into a partnership with two men named Hans Godfritsen and Henry Warner in the operation of a store on the riverfront. It was not a success. With the three large mines shut down, the riverboats appeared only sporadically to ferry out the comparatively meager ore shipments dug out by independent miners. Eventually Warner and Piette quarreled loudly in a tavern. The next day Warner disappeared. A pale and frightened Godfritsen abandoned his interest in the store before nightfall and rode off toward Yuma.

This was too much for the remaining miners in the town to take. Again there are two versions of the tale. The more lurid tells of half a dozen miners surrounding Piette's store and calling for him to come out. When he refused, the attackers emptied their guns into the small frame store, and, when they were sure that Piette was dead, they dragged out his body and threw it into the Colorado River. The other story relates that Piette was visited by a delegation of irate citizens and ordered out of the community. If he returned, they warned, he would be hanged. In either event, Piette disappeared, as had Nash and Warner, and with his disappearance, the murders and mysterious vanishings ended.

None of the three mines ever were reopened. Not long ago, the *Mohave County Miners,* a weekly newspaper, reported "a deep silence lies over all that once was a wild and lawless spot. A curse seems upon the place. Yet these mines contained millions of wealth. Their product is estimated at about $3 million."

The gold is there. So may be the ghost of William Piette.

HONOR AMONG THIEVES

In 1891 a large group of bandits raided the city of Monterrey, Mexico. They held off an army detachment and police in the city, killing a few men while they looted several banks and the cathedral of more treasure than usually was carried in a Spanish galleon. One semiofficial estimate of the loot includes $1 million in diamonds, 39 bars of gold worth $600,000, $90,000 worth of silver coins, plus an undetermined amount of gold statuary, and stacks of gold coins. The value of the booty exceeded by far the wildest estimates of its planners. The raid was a catalyst for a fantastic series of double crosses and counter double crosses and was directly responsible for the naming of Skeleton Canyon in the Peloncillo Mountains on the border of Arizona and New Mexico.

The raid was the idea of Curly Bill Brocius, the leader of a small gang of cutthroats who spent a considerable amount of time in Silver City, New Mexico. For several months they had been preying upon stagecoaches and lone travelers in Arizona, but the rewards had been meager for the risks involved.

Curly Bill called a meeting in his cabin outside Silver City. Those present included Jim Hughes, fluent in Spanish and ranking next to Curly Bill in the gang's hierarchy, Zwing Hunt, Billy Grounds, and Doc Neal. A few years earlier Hughes was identified as the murderer of several people during a stagecoach holdup in Texas and slipped across the Mexican border only a few hoofbeats ahead of a pursuing posse. For a while he lived in Monterrey, where he picked up his proficiency in Spanish and a slowly increasing awareness of the wealth of the city. Hughes later drifted west, but stayed well below the border. In Sonora, he ran across the notorious Mexican bandit José Estrada. Hughes promptly was extended professional courtesy, from one desperado to another, and for several months Hughes roamed the state of Sonora with the Mexican bandit and his gang. One day, the bandits veered to the north to escape a pursuing army patrol, and Hughes slipped across the border back into the United States where, a short time later, he joined up with Curly Bill Brocius.

At the meeting in Silver City, Hughes nostalgically recalled his days in Mexico and, during the course of his conversation, mentioned the richness of Monterrey.

"Why don't we raid it?" Curly Bill suggested.

His suggestion was received enthusiastically. A moment later, the first double cross was conceived by Hughes. If the raid were to be carried out by non-Mexicans, they would easily be recognized as such. Besides the difficulty in getting out of Mexico, the magnitude of the crime might trigger an unfavorable reaction from the United States government. Mexican help was needed, Hughes argued, for the raid must be considered a Mexican operation. Therefore, they would enlist the bandits of José Estrada to conduct the mission.

"Estrada's not going to give us anything just because we gave him an idea," Curly Bill objected.

Hughes had an answer for Brocius. Because of the magnitude of the crime, the Mexican authorities would send an army after the raiders. The only thing that would stop them would be the United States border. In addition, Estrada would have trouble in disposing of his loot in Mexico. Therefore, Hughes would go with Estrada on the raid, travel with the band back to Sonora, then guide them across the border to the sanctuary of the hideout in the Peloncillo Mountains. "By the time we get to the canyon east of Sloan's Ranch, Estrada will be very tired," Hughes pointed out. "I will ride on ahead, and then we will ambush them there," he said.

"And I will remain in Silver City so no one can blame us when they find the Mexicans' bodies," Curly Bill added.

The plan was endorsed unanimously. Time has obscured how long it took to bring the raid to fruition. Hughes went to Sonora and found Estrada to be as enthusiastic about the venture as were his co-conspirators across the border. Although it was many hundred miles from northwestern Sonora to Monterrey, the logistics of the raid were not difficult. The land was sparsely populated and arid for the most part so their trail would be difficult to follow if they had a sufficient head start. Also, it was as customary for Mexicans to flee across the border into the United States to avoid capture by Mexican law enforcement officials as it was for American desperadoes to slip into Mexico when the chase became too close. Thus, Estrada and Hughes reasoned correctly that the pursuit following the raid would be to the nearest point north of the border. It would not occur to anyone that the quarry would be racing west, remaining in Mexico.

The raid was carried out with great success. Estrada, his band, and Hughes pillaged the community for almost three hours. The telegraph wires were cut. Four police officers and an undetermined number of soldiers were slain before the raiders successfully penned them in a barrack. After looting the banks and the cathedral and stealing some pack mules, the raiders vanished.

There is no record of the long overland journey to Sonora. Some reports contend that the Estrada gang buried part of the loot outside of Monterrey and went back for it several months later. Other reports, which are probably more accurate, assert that the bandits fled to the west as planned and were successful in eluding the army patrols sent after them. It is known that several weeks later, the Estrada gang and Hughes, accompanied by a mule train carrying the booty, entered the United States through the Arizona territory along an old smugglers' trail that cut through the Animas Valley.

The gang made camp in an isolated section of the Peloncillo Mountain foothills near the juncture of what is now known as Skeleton Creek and the South Fork Skeleton Creek. Hughes rode on ahead to Silver City where the plans for the double cross were gone over once again. Nothing could go wrong, Hughes promised. Most of the Estrada gang had been paid off in Sonora so, in addition to Estrada, there were only a dozen Mexicans with whom to contend.

Curly Bill remained in Silver City as planned. Neal, Grounds, and Hunt accompanied Hughes to a point a few miles from the Estrada camp. Here they set up their ambush in a canyon so narrow that a pack train would have to pass through it in single file. When the men were positioned, Hughes rode back to his old friend Estrada.

A few hours later the pack mules were loaded, the camp was struck, and the train headed for Silver City with Hughes leading the way. It was late afternoon when the caravan entered the canyon. Hughes started the slaughter when he stopped his horse and fired a bullet into the head of Estrada. A few moments later all of the Mexicans had been killed. The ambush did not go as planned, however. The sound of the gunfire echoed loudly throughout the defile, and the treasure-laden mules panicked at the noise and bolted.

The North American outlaws set off in pursuit. The only way they could stop the fleeing animals was to shoot them. All but two of the animals were killed in the canyon—one was shot about a mile outside the canyon entrance and the other disappeared, last seen heading in the direction of Geronimo's Peak.

The killing of the pack animals posed a problem. There was no way to transport the Monterrey booty to the hideout in the Peloncillo Mountains. Someone had to return to Silver City to get more mules or oxen, and someone had to remain to gather up the treasure, as well as guard it, and bury the dead. While this was being discussed, one of the outlaws questioned the need for Curly Bill's participation in the division of the loot. Although nominally the leader of the gang, he had done nothing to earn a portion of this treasure. It was unanimously decided that Jim Hughes should go back to Silver City and tell Curly Bill that Estrada had escaped. If Curly Bill did not believe him, Hughes would kill him. Hughes then would return with oxen or mules to carry the treasure away. Unfortunately for him, Hughes agreed to this plan.

Hughes was barely out of sight when Neal, Hunt, and

Grounds convened another meeting. It would take a few days for Hughes to make a round trip to Silver City, more if he came back with oxen. There really was no need for him to be cut in on a division of the booty. Doc Neal could buy an ox team from a ranch much closer, and the three of them could load the treasure and be long gone before Hughes returned. The gullible Doc Neal thought this an excellent plan. Taking several gold coins from one of the packs on a dead mule, he cantered off to the west in search of an ox team.

Zwing Hunt and Billy Grounds then proceeded to dig a large hole in a small level spot, about a mile east of the massacre site, in what is now known as Skeleton Canyon. Estimates vary as to how much of the booty they succeeded in burying. The smallest estimate is $80,000. The highest says almost half of the loot wound up buried in Skeleton Canyon.

Doc Neal returned within two days leading a team of oxen. He noticed that many of the treasure pouches had been opened during his absence and that obviously many were missing from the packs of the dead mules. Neal, however, was smart enough to say nothing to his double-crossing companions as they loaded up the ox cart.

For two days, or about fifty miles, the three outlaws drove the oxen east toward New Mexico. Then, near the Arizona-New Mexico border, they veered north into the Peloncillo Mountains. It was then that Doc Neal noticed that Hunt and Grounds often conversed in whispers. Being a practical man, Neal assumed the worst—that his life expectancy would indeed be short if he remained with his companions. Consequently, when an opportunity arose, he galloped back down the mountain. The hail of bullets that accompanied his flight confirmed his suspicions, but he escaped unscathed.

Neal went directly to Silver City, New Mexico, where he found Hughes sleeping in Curly Bill's cabin. Curly Bill was serving a week's sentence in jail for slugging a deputy sheriff in the course of a barroom brawl. Hughes, therefore, had not had an opportunity to tell the gang leader of Estrada's alleged escape. Hughes, understandably, was upset when he learned from Neal of the perfidy of Hunt and Grounds. He and Neal devised a new plan. As soon as Curly Bill was released they would go after Hunt and Grounds. The booty then would be divided in three parts between Curly Bill, Hughes, and Neal.

When Curly Bill was let out of jail he was met by Hughes and Neal. The three men went to a saloon where Hughes told Curly Bill of the double cross pulled by the other two members of the gang. Curly Bill became furious. So great was his anger that he lost control of himself, and when a young barmaid accidently brushed his chair, he whipped out his gun and shot her. Women were scarce in Silver City, and the killing of one was a truly heinous offense.

The three outlaws immediately fled the town, but a posse was after them in less than a half-hour and caught up with them in the New Mexican town of Shakespeare. In the ensuing gunfight, Doc Neal was fatally shot. Curly Bill Brocius and Jim Hughes were captured and immediately hanged from a rafter in the dining room of the Pioneer Hotel in Shakespeare.

Meanwhile, Hunt and Grounds had buried the rest of the Monterrey treasure, except for as many gold coins as they could carry, and had moved on to Tombstone, Arizona. Word of the mysterious massacre had spread throughout the Southwest by this time, but most thought the victims were Mexican smugglers killed by Indians. The two surviving members of Curly Bill's gang spent their money wildly on booze and women.

Grounds had a girl friend in Charleston, a small community a short distance from Tombstone, but he was not the only man in her life. She had a much closer liaison with the town butcher. The butcher, however, did not have as much money as Billy Grounds. This posed a problem for the young woman. If Billy's wealth was temporary, then she would choose the butcher. But if Billy was indeed a man of lasting substance, then she would choose him.

She finally overcame Billy Grounds's reluctance to discuss the source of his riches and his net worth by getting him gloriously drunk. While lying in bed at the side of his beloved, Billy told all. After Billy left for Tombstone on the following day, his girl friend relayed the news to the butcher. When Grounds returned to Charleston that evening, the irate butcher went to Tombstone to tell Sheriff William Breckenridge of the two mass murderers living in his jurisdiction. The woman saw him leave and, in turn, confessed to Grounds what she had done. Grounds immediately raced into Tombstone, found Zwing Hunt and told him the bad news. While Hunt ran to the bank to withdraw the funds he had deposited, Grounds took the time to write a letter to his mother in San Antonio, Texas. He wrote:

Dear Ma,

    I am coming home and will be on my way within the hour. I am tired of this wild life. I wanted to lay my head again in your lap and have you run your fingers through my hair as you did when I was a little tot and came to you with my troubles. I have $80,000 buried which I came by honestly. I will get

this and be home and buy a ranch near Santone and
you can live in comfort the rest of your days.

Your loving boy,
Billy

P.S. I am charged with crimes I did not commit and
may not get home. So I am enclosing a map showing
just where this treasure is buried so you and Sis can
get it if I do not get home.

Billy Grounds mailed the letter from Tombstone as he
and Zwing Hunt rode out of town. There was no immediate
sign of a chase, and, after they covered about ten miles, they
thought it safe to spend the night in an empty bunkhouse on a
ranch owned by a man named Chandler. It was a mistake. The
next morning shortly after dawn they were awakened by a
cry from Sheriff Breckenridge to come out with their hands
up. Breckenridge was accompanied by two deputies named
Gillespie and Young.

Grounds and Hunt charged out of the bunkhouse with
guns blazing. Gillespie was shot dead, and Young was felled
by a bullet which shattered his leg. The sheriff then shot
Grounds in the head with a shotgun and Hunt through the
chest with his revolver. Both of the outlaws were carried
back to Tombstone in one of the ranch buckboards. Grounds
died in the wagon and was buried in the Tombstone Cemetery.
Hunt was placed in the local hospital and was expected to die.

Zwing Hunt asked that his brother Hugh be notified of
his pending demise, and a short time later Hugh Hunt arrived
in Tombstone from Tucson. His stay was brief. Immediately
after his arrival he rented a horse and buggy, and after dark,
in some unknown manner, smuggled Zwing out of the hospital. The escape was not discovered until the following morning,

and the trail was difficult to follow.

Breckenridge, however, was a stubborn man and within a few days deduced from the various reports that came in that the Hunt brothers were heading for the massacre sight in Skeleton Canyon. He resumed the chase. A few miles to the west of where Estrada had been killed, the sheriff and his deputies came across a freshly dug grave at the foot of an oak tree. Carved into the bark of the tree was the name Zwing Hunt. The officers unearthed the grave and found the body of Zwing inside. The men covered up the grave and returned to Tombstone. Hugh Hunt was not worth pursuing.

The map and letter that Bill Grounds sent to his mother on the day before his death are reported still to be in good condition and in the possession of Grounds's sister's son who lives in San Antonio, Texas. No attempt has been made to recover the Monterrey booty by Grounds's descendants.

Many others have searched for it, however, and many have found gold and silver coins, probably scattered by the bolting pack mules, in Skeleton Canyon near the Arizona-New Mexico border. Weldon Heald, writing in *Desert* magazine in 1951, says that Hunt, just before he died, wrote out detailed instructions on how to find the treasure site, which he stated is at the foot of Davis Mountain. Heald repeats the intricate directions, but points out that they are worthless since there is no Davis Mountain in this area of the country.

At this writing the oak tree under which Hunt is buried still stands. A short distance to the east and to the north of Skeleton Creek is the massacre site, and in this area a part of the treasure was buried. The rest of the Monterrey booty is two days' trip by oxen to the east. It should be remembered that everyone who has possessed it since it was looted in Monterrey has died violently.

176

EPILOGUE

The theme of this volume has concerned treasures of the West that have yet to be found, or, if the location is known, have yet to be recovered. Many skeptics of treasure legends dismiss the existence of these valuable caches on the grounds that if such treasure ever had been buried or lost, they would eventually have been found.

Some treasures may well have been found, and the finder kept the knowledge of his discovery to himself. The location of other treasures has been determined but, for one reason or another, it has been impossible to recover them. The foundered Manila galleon on Nehalem Spit in Oregon is one such case. Some treasure tales are most improbable, particularly those that we mentioned earlier that start out with a deathbed confession.

But before anyone becomes discouraged by these low probabilities, he should consider the case of the late Shorty Wilcox of Colorado. He learned of a treasure from the lips of a dying man, hurried to its location, and found it beyond his physical and financial resources to recover it. Yet, within the passage of a few weeks, he obtained possession of this treasure and spent the remainder of his life playing the stock market and living comfortably in a plush suite in the Brown Palace Hotel in Denver, Colorado.

In the early 1880s, when Shorty Wilcox was in his mid-thirties, Colorado was in the throes of a crime wave. Holdup men swooped down in gangs on banks, saloons, and stores. The state was second only to California in the number of stagecoach robberies tallied. Among those who preyed on stagecoaches was a sadistic trio of young men who killed passengers without reason, and who, for a period of more than four years, left behind no clues as to their identity.

Shortly before this trio began its operations, three young men filed claim upon the Black Prince Mine in Summit County, Colorado. The mine had been abandoned several years earlier after an explosion tapped an underground spring and flooded the main shaft under eighty feet of water. The three new operators were unfriendly. They bought their supplies in nearby Breckenridge and usually stopped in a tavern on their way out of town. Here they spoke only in monosyllables and only to each other. Their names were known from the claim filing: Alva Davis, Rick Johnson, and Max Smith. They appeared to be making the small mine profitable, for they paid their bills and occasionally brought in ore to be assayed. No one knew how they had drained the water from the main shaft. No questions were answered, and, if a person passed too close to the Black Prince Mine, he was turned away. The merchants and residents of Breckenridge, along with other miners in the area, became used to the taciturn trio and ignored them. More than four years passed before the three became suspects in the wave of stagecoach robberies and killings, and this was not because anyone had become suspicious of their cover.

Another stagecoach robbery had occurred near Alma in

adjacent Park County. One of the gunman emptied his revolver into the coach as he rode away, killing one of the passengers and wounding two others. A posse was quickly formed to give chase; it followed the trail into Summit County. Previously, when outlaws escaped into an adjoining county, a pursuing posse abandoned the chase because the lawmen had passed out of their jurisdiction. In this instance, however, the Park County sheriff continued into Summit County, detaching one member of the posse to ride on to the Summit County sheriff to explain what was going on. The Summit County sheriff responded by forming still another posse and joining the chase.

A short time later, the two posses formed a tight circle around the Black Prince Mine where the trail had ended, and presently discovered that their quarry had fled. Although they searched for more than a day, the men failed to pick up the outlaws' trail again. Their only consolation was that they now had a fairly good idea as to the identity of the killers.

The following day the Park County posse cantered into a small canyon north of Alma and stumbled into the middle of a holdup of a Wells Fargo stagecoach. The gun battle was quick and deadly. When it was over two of the masked outlaws were dead, along with one member of the posse and one stagecoach passenger. The third outlaw escaped. The bodies of the dead outlaws were taken into Alma where they were subsequently identified as those of Alva Davis and Rick Johnson.

Some twenty years later Shorty Wilcox arrived in Breckenridge. For several years he had worked in the large Orizaba gold mine in Cripple Creek until he suffered a permanent injury to his legs when the shoring of a drift tunnel collapsed upon them. He built a cabin on the outskirts of the town and picked up small amounts of money from the women of the community in the role of a handyman. No job was too small or too menial for Shorty Wilcox. He was always polite and cheerful. The wife of the superintendent of the Orizaba Mine described him "as neat and clean as a new needle and with the disposition of a minister."

When Shorty Wilcox became sick, which appeared to happen regularly, the women of the community supplied him with food and took turns nursing him back to health. After these bouts, he would limp around to the homes of his benefactors, personally thanking each one, begging for some small chore to perform as a sign of his appreciation. For almost five years Shorty Wilcox lived this way, until one night a stranger arrived at Shorty's cabin on the outskirts of town.

The stranger arrived on foot, knocked feebly on the door, then collapsed when Shorty opened the door. Shorty dragged him to his bed and made some tea. The beverage restored some color to the stranger's pallid cheeks. "I'm Max Smith," he said presently. "Does my name mean anything to you?"

Shorty shook his head. A quarter-century had passed since the abandoned Black Prince Mine had been used as a bandit hideout.

Max Smith sighed, then clutched his chest. When the pain subsided, his breathing was fast and shallow. He began talking in a rapid monotone, telling Shorty of the robberies and the large sums of money that had been taken. After his partners had been killed, Smith went on, he had fled to Santa Fe in New Mexico territory. Here he had been caught during a burglary and sentenced to twenty-five years in prison. Immediately upon his release, he had headed for the Black Prince Mine.

"I've been up there for the past month trying to figure

out how to get it out," he continued. "There's no way it can be done."

Shorty poured his visitor another cup of tea. He waited.

"We put fifty thousand dollars in gold coins, all from the Denver Mint, into a strong box," Smith said after a while. "When the posse started to get close, we tossed it down the main shaft. It was the savings of almost four years."

"Now, why can't you get it out?" Shorty asked curiously.

"Cause the shaft has got more than eighty feet of water in it." Max Smith again clutched his chest and grimaced in pain. "More than four years' savings," he moaned.

All through the night, Shorty remained at the side of Max Smith. Toward dawn, his uninvited guest slipped into a coma, and an hour or so later Shorty limped into Breckinridge to fetch the doctor. When they returned to the cabin, Max Smith was dead.

"Just stumbled against the door last night," Shorty told the doctor. "Said his name was Smith and that he was sick."

The body of the stranger, unrecognized and unclaimed, was buried in an unmarked grave in Breckenridge. A few days later Shorty Wilcox told Mrs. Virginia Petit, wife of the superintendent of the Orizaba Mine, that he was planning to spend more time mining, adding that he thought he would put in a claim for the abandoned Black Prince Mine. When she told her husband he laughed, commenting that Shorty was losing his mind in his old age.

About two weeks later the women of Breckenridge realized that their favorite man-about-town had disappeared. A delegation was dispatched to Shorty's cabin. Shorty was an unusually neat and tidy man, but now there was dust on the table and floor to indicate that its occupant had been gone for a considerable time. Someone recalled Shorty's plan to stake out the old abandoned Black Prince Mine. The next day some of the more energetic women of Breckenridge rode up to the Black Prince. Their fears appeared to be justified. Two planks had been laid across the opening of the main shaft, and on one of these planks was a half-eaten sandwich and half a cup of coffee. Peering over the side of the shaft, the ladies could see the water below. Floating on top of the water was a straw hat that Shorty Wilcox always wore outdoors.

The ladies hurried back to town. Virginia Petit led the group that started the movement to retrieve Shorty's body and return it to Breckenridge where it could be buried with the proper religious rites. The pressure was too great for the practical men of the community to resist, particularly as Mrs. Petit was aware of the existence of a powerful pump kept at the Orizaba Mine.

It took many men several days to haul the heavy pump across the mountains to the Black Prince Mine. There was no power to run the pump and it took a few more days for the men, working in relays, one man on each end of a rocker arm, to pump the water out of the shaft. When the shaft eventually was cleared, however, there was no sign of a body.

While the men and women were mulling over this unexpected development, Shorty Wilcox limped up the trail into the camp. His lined face reflected a combination of anger and surprise. "What are you doing on my property?" he demanded.

If there had not been women present, Shorty Wilcox might have been hanged immediately from a nearby tree by the tired men. There was not a male volunteer present who did not know that he had been tricked into clearing the shaft. The women, however, apparently believed Shorty's story that he had impulsively crossed the mountains to visit a friend at another mine. After Shorty pointed out that he had not requested any help and that everyone present was trespassing, the volunteers packed up and left.

The women did not lose their concern over the well-being of Shorty Wilcox. On the following day, Mrs. Paul Priest and some unidentified friends rode out to the Black Prince Mine to take Shorty a basket of food. An A-frame had been built over the mouth of the shaft and lying on the ground was a block and tackle and a muddy cast-iron hook. But once again, Shorty Wilcox had disappeared. The women returned to Breckenridge. The men of the community were uninterested in his whereabouts. For several weeks the women made periodic visits to Shorty's cabin, but the miner never returned to his small cabin on the outskirts of town.

Several months later Mrs. Priest and her husband checked into the Brown Palace Hotel in Denver. As they turned away from the desk after registering, they saw Shorty Wilcox. He was a picture of sartorial splendor as he limped across the thick-carpeted floor to the open door. An astonished Mr. Priest made some inquiries around the city. The records of banks at the turn of the century were slightly less confidential than they are today, and Priest quickly discovered that Shorty Wilcox had deposited about $50,000 in gold coins in one of the banks a few days after he had last been seen at the Black Prince Mine.

Priest also discovered that Shorty lived in a suite in the Brown Palace. He tried on this and subsequent trips to visit him, but Shorty Wilcox had lost all interest in his former neighbors from Breckenridge. He invested his money wisely and lived luxuriously until his death a few years later.

Shorty Wilcox took the words of a dying man seriously, overcame insurmountable odds, and recovered a treasure despite the fact that he was crippled and an old man.

Most legends have some basis in fact. The treasures we have described probably exist, and someone, someday, probably will find them.